COMPANY GROWTH BY ACQUISITION MAKES DOLLARS & SENSE

COMPANY GROWTH BY ACQUISITION MAKES DOLLARS & SENSE

John Martinka

Company Growth by Acquisition Makes Dollars & Sense

John Martinka

ISBN: 1975710622
ISBN 13: 9781975710620
Library of Congress Control Number: 2017913416
CreateSpace Independent Publishing Platform
North Charleston, South Carolina

CONTENTS

PREFACE

I realized since the 2013 publication of my very successful book *Buying a Business That Makes You Rich*, I have worked on about a dozen deals that were *growth by acquisition*. It's obviously a popular subject for small and midsized business owners, not just large corporations and private equity firms.

While all of these deals were focused on growth, there were also a variety of other reasons, as explained in detail in chapter 2. The reasons included more employees, geographic expansion, new product lines, new distribution channels, and a more diverse group of customers. You'll read stories about some of these deals at the end of every chapter.

The next logical step was this book, a book focused on why and how to grow by acquisition, for small to midsized companies. Because of this focus, you won't see anything on if you should make the plunge into business ownership (you have). You will see a lot of reasons you should consider this strategy as well as how to best achieve a successful acquisition.

My good friend and client Rick Locke told me that while he thought it would be tough to have a title using the word "quest," he recommended I try to find a way to use it. He was right; it was tough, and I couldn't get a catchy title with it. But he makes an excellent point, as growth by acquisition is a quest you must navigate. The definition of "quest" is "a long or arduous search for something" (Oxford *Living* Dictionaries, oxforddictionaries.com). As you read the book and especially the chapter-ending stories, you'll realize it is a quest that when completed can yield great results.

Growth by acquisition also feeds very well into the subject of my second book, *If They Can Sell Pet Rocks, Why Can't You Sell Your Business (for What You Want)?* As we'll see, having a larger company increases your firm's value and your exit options.

Note I rotate between using the words "he" or "she" as I describe situations to keep it simple.

One thing I am sure you will like is every chapter ends with a short story or two about clients who grew by acquisition. Read their words about why they did it and what they liked about it; I hope you benefit from their tips for others embarking on this journey.

ACKNOWLEDGMENTS

I t wasn't the easiest thing to choose a title. *Growth by Acquisition* on its own is blah. Something esoteric doesn't convey the subject, and therefore, this book wouldn't be found during online searches.

I'd like to thank two people for the title. First, thank you to John Kaminski with One Accord Partners in Kirkland, Washington. While we planned and coproduced a seminar on this topic, John came up with the "makes dollars and sense" part of the title. My good friend and "Partner" On-Call Network cofounder, Ted Leverette, made sure the title specified "company growth by acquisition." Again, thanks to both of them.

CHAPTER 1

WHY?

Why questions are very popular with marketing experts.

- Why do customers buy from you?
- Why do they pay what they pay so you can make a profit (this is your competitive advantage)?
- Why do your employees work for you?
- And for this book, why should you consider buying another company (i.e., growth by acquisition)?

The big-picture answer is simple. You buy another business to have a larger company, immediate growth, and more profit. All the reasons given in chapter 2 are subsets of this. If you don't want a larger, more profitable company, there is no reason to consider an acquisition. In other words, you must not only desire but also be focused on growth and the future.

Why Are You a Business Owner?

Let's go back to when you started or bought your current company. Why did you do it? Which of the following reasons was it?

- Benefitting yourself (from your hard and smart work)
- Challenge
- Control
- Creativity

- Freedom
- Flexibility
- Implementing your idea
- Independence
- Money
- Fun (a great reason to take the plunge into business ownership)

What is it now? Based on client input, my first guess is money and challenge top the list, along with "work less" if you can get more management depth.

What about being a savior to a distressed business? You know as well as I do there are a lot of lousy businesses out there. Here's one formula for creating a lousy business, a scenario in which you should be interested:

Take a person fed up with being an employee, or the corporate world is fed up with her. Add a lot of "product knowledge." Forget about business, management, sales, or leadership skills, and have the person start a business. Customers come to this person because her product is so good, and, at least initially, the price is very good.

As the business grows, the owner spends less time on her passion (the product) and more with the people, and it's frustrating. So the business becomes a low-paying, lousy job with a lousy boss.

You become the solution. You buy the business, get the owner out of her rut, give her a job she likes, or let her retire, and you increase sales, without (much) added overhead.

Control Your Risk"

What about reducing risk? All other things being equal, a $5 million business has more risk than a $10 million business, which has more risk than a $25 million business, and so on. By less risk, I'm referring to things such as lower dependencies, including the following:

- A greater chance of customer diversity (versus customer-concentration issues)
- Lower odds of one key employee who would create a bottleneck if he left
- Having management team depth
- Most importantly, less reliance on the owner

The last point is key. One of the things you will fear as a buyer (and a buyer will fear when it's time to buy your business) is how you fill in the blank in the following statement: the owner is _____. Some of the fill-in-the-blank options you want to be wary of are the following:

- The only one who can program the machine
- The person with the key customer relationships
- The only person who understands the intricacies of the bidding process

I think you get my point, which is as you grow, you can add depth, which reduces risk. To control risk and grow, this is what you need.

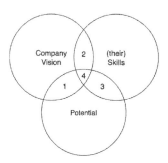

The preceding diagram shows the following:

1. A company with vision and potential will fail if the buyer doesn't have the right skills.
2. If the buyer has the skills and the business has vision (strategy), but the business has no potential, it will stagnate.

3. Skills and potential without a vision mean the buyer will be lost, chasing too much and achieving little.
4. When all three elements are present, the sale, transition, and future of the company will likely be successful.

When to Buy Another One

Business ownership is not for everybody. Most people are content with being an employee, doing their jobs, and collecting a paycheck. Nothing wrong with that. As an owner, you know how important good employees are to the success of your company.

In the same vein, buying another company is not for everybody, despite all the headlines about mergers and acquisitions (M&A) activity in the middle market and public-company market. Even if it is for you, a very important question is, when is the right time? Some of that is happenstance, as the following story demonstrates.

Here's How It Works

Fred bought a great business with profits, growth (every year during the Great Recession), a solid customer base, and a team of "experts" to handle the work.

About fifteen months after his deal closed, through my normal day-to-day activities, I found another company in his industry, which had a motivated seller (for personal reasons). Fred wanted to buy multiple companies, but the plan was to wait two to three years.

However, this was too good a situation to pass up. He at least had to look at it. What he saw was a firm with different customers; a similar but different product; the opportunity for geographic expansion; and the ability to consolidate functions, to reduce overhead, and to have higher-level people (e.g., an in-house accountant versus a bookkeeper).

He liked what he saw and hit it off with the seller. His bank liked the deal, and in less than two years, it was 50 percent larger. There's more about Fred's story at the end of chapter 2.

For most owners, it's not happenstance but a planned strategy. It has to do with things such as where you are on the growth curve, your capital, your ability and desire to devote time to implementing the strategy, and your business's seasonality. It's a mistake to take on an acquisition if the timing isn't right.

There's another factor, and that's where the company is on the legacy scale when you arrive on the scene. The further up the scale, which is presented in the following diagram, the higher the price, in theory. Is that what you want? I don't know, and you might not know until you see it.

As the diagram shows, the sweet spot is generally between where the owner is a manager (versus a doer) and when she is a true CEO. The reason being the company is beyond the start-up phase, and there's still plenty of room to add value.

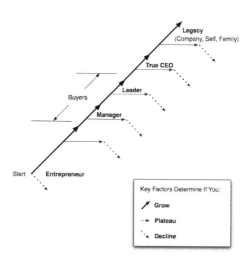

Why, Again?

The timing of an acquisition is one thing. More important is, does it make sense? Not does it make sense *now*, but does it make sense at all? Some businesses might not lend themselves to this strategy. Some owners aren't interested. But if you have the bandwidth, good target companies, and the willingness, it can be a wonderful way to grow, as you'll see.

Why They Made an Acquisition

John Hoyt is the founder and CEO of Picture Source NW in Seattle (www.picture-source.com), one of the nation's leading providers of art for residential and commercial customers. Most recently, John acquired Somerset Studios in North Carolina, one of a handful of acquisitions he has made.

These are the three things John likes most about acquisitions:

- The adventure (of the process)—it's thrilling to him to find a company that adds value to Picture Source and put a deal together.
- The increased energy level—everybody gets jazzed as it comes together and during the transition. He's found it brings together not only his team but also the employees of the other company.
- The culture improvement—he's found this brings everybody together, and the results spill over to the other aspects of the business.

When I asked why he made these acquisitions, his answer sounded like the perfect segue to chapter 2 as he rattled off five reasons.

1. New distribution channel
2. Location (i.e., geographic expansion, which can also lower overall costs; having an East Coast location saves Picture Source a lot of money on shipping)
3. Talent, especially on the creative side

4. New account base, customers he couldn't get without the products and channels
5. New capabilities, in his case, meaning more products (e.g., with the acquisition of Somerset, he acquired an operation producing original artwork)

John's tip for others is to hire outside advisors and use your team to avoid problems.

CHAPTER 2

NINETEEN REASONS TO GROW BY ACQUISITION

The Cake: Sixteen Solid Reasons (in Alphabetical Order)

1. Acquire great talent, including the seller
2. Assets are cheaper as a package
3. Competitive advantage (fill a weakness)
4. Dependencies reduced
5. Diamonds in the rough
6. Diversify your product offerings
7. Easy money
8. Integration is easier
9. Location, location, location
10. Make a competitor go away
11. Psychology (employees like to be part of a winner, a growing firm, like sports fans jumping on the winning team's bandwagon)
12. Risk is a lot lower
13. Overhead the same, volume higher
14. Synergy
15. Technologies
16. Vendor-relationship strategies

The Icing: The Top Three (Not in Alphabetical Order)

17. Customers (efficiency versus making more calls)
18. Yes, we can!
19. The bigger you are...the better

The Cake: Sixteen Solid Reasons

Acquire Great Talent

Good employees are hard to find and often are not in the job market. Just talk to any executive recruiter. While all buyers want capable employees, most strategic buyers (that's you) also prefer to see a solid management team in place.

Great employees with industry knowledge and experience are even scarcer in the job market (than others). When you are looking for great salespeople, I believe this is amplified; they are hard to find. They won't change jobs if they've got a good thing going. Here are some statistics from an executive recruiter, which explain why it's tough to find good people.

- Eighty-two percent of employed people aren't searching for a job.
- Leadership, or the lack thereof, is the top reason management people switch jobs (not money).
- Forty-six percent of millennials left their last jobs because of the lack of career growth.

If you acquire a company and create an atmosphere of growth, those employees will want to stay. While I can't comment on the culture in all companies, I do know many small, family-owned businesses have owners who are coasting. They are doing very well, they aren't working too hard, and they don't want to disrupt the nice moneymaking system they have.

Real-Life Story

One of my clients had trouble keeping a licensed person. His strategy was to acquire a small contractor to head up his contracting department. The story we painted was incredible, especially for an owner sick and tired of all the admin work that accompanies running a very small business.

The picture of the advantages included the buyer taking over all the administration (all financial aspects, scheduling, purchasing, and more), gaining the ability to grow a division, mentoring people, and receiving a full-benefit package, including vacation, medical insurance, 401(k) match, steady income, and so on.

Again, if you can't hire them, it may make sense to buy them.

The employees may be younger and have more energy and ideas on how to grow and challenge themselves and the firm. To the seller, this could mean a bigger payday but a corresponding risk of slightly lower profits if the ideas don't work or a temporary profit reduction as there's an investment in the new idea. In addition, often, the owner's skills have been maxed out. They just can't grow it anymore.

Maybe you keep the owner on the team. You buy the business, and keep his wealth of product and customer knowledge on the team. You get productivity, and the seller is happy to be rid of the management responsibilities.

Warning—some sellers can't accept working for someone else after years of being in charge.

Real-Life Story

I once had two clients (coincidentally, both in Los Angeles and both distributors) who hired me to find companies in their specific industries. The prime motivator for both was to acquire great salespeople. They needed people with industry knowledge and experience, and they were having trouble finding people willing to change jobs. Buying another company with a good sales staff made more sense than trying to steal employees.

Assets Are Cheaper as a Package

Tangible assets are a sunk cost. Once you have them—whether vehicles, machines, forklifts, or space—you have the cost or payments. You need to make them efficient. All businesses struggle with this for both tangible and human assets.

At some point, you must buy a new machine (or hire a new person) because of overcapacity on current equipment, people are working too much overtime, or some other reason. However, once you buy that piece of equipment, your capacity increases and your utilization drops. You must generate more sales to get the equipment running at a profitable rate.

Wouldn't it be nice if the equipment, like people, came with sales orders? Of course it would, and that's why buying another company can be a good way to get needed equipment with corresponding customers. As the header for this section states, these assets can be cheaper as a package (as opposed to buying new or used assets that don't come with customers).

As emphasized in the previous section, you also get the employees who know how to operate the equipment (or provide the service). As I write this, there's a shortage of qualified people in the marketplace. I don't care if it's machinists, salespeople, tradespeople, or something else. Owners have told me they can't find qualified people or people who can pass a background check or a drug test. An acquisition just might be the answer to this problem.

Competitive Advantage

Door-to-Door Storage created an industry in the late 1990s. It was the idea of mobile storage (deliver a pod, load it, and take it back to a climate-controlled warehouse). They raised angel financing and venture capital financing and gave birth to an industry.

But the competitive advantage they had was low, as were the barriers of entry. It wasn't long after they launched the business that I met a person doing the same thing with a different name. Now it's a saturated industry with almost every moving, warehouse, and rental company (like U-Haul) offering similar services.

Contrast this scenario with these examples.

- An environmental engineering firm that has built a reputation of doing great work, on time, and at a fair price, becoming the go-to firm in their market with many, many law firms (environmental attorneys)
- A software company whose product fixes the gaps in major server-software programs
- The machine shop with its own proprietary product that does what no other product does for its aerospace customers
- The outsource HR service company that keeps small businesses compliant with all the moving-target rules and regulations at one-third to one-half the cost of the full-time employee they replaced

What is your target and your competitive advantage? Whether it be quality, value, service, intellectual property, or something else, this is your opportunity to combine forces and exploit them.

Dependencies Reduced

Dependencies are a huge issue in most small businesses. By being larger, you can reduce dependencies in most or all of the following:

1. Customers
2. Employees
3. Management abilities

4. Product
5. Owner

Not too much explanation is needed. You have more customers over your expanded revenue base, more employees, deeper management, less product concentration, and, most important, more talent to take a load off the owner. As previously mentioned, an owner dependency is often the brightest red flag for most profitable small businesses. Integrating another operation into yours can reduce the owner dependency in the seller's business.

Diamonds in the Rough

This may mean buying a loser, it may mean buying a struggling business (personal income to the owner but no real profit), or it could mean buying a business where you can see things that can be done to make it more than it is now.

Often, the mediocre business has no options other than to struggle along, close the doors, or sell to another business. Rarely will individuals or other financial buyers (those needing an income from the business) buy a loser. That means their options are very limited, as only a small percentage of companies ever consider growth by acquisition, which makes it an even stronger strategy for those who do.

This can be a good opportunity and at a low cost. Perhaps you could even purchase on an earn-out basis (nonguaranteed payments to the seller based on sales or profits or the increase of sales and profits). And these can still be win-win deals. You get volume, people, and other benefits, and the seller gets more money for the company she wouldn't have otherwise gotten (or gets some money when she wouldn't have gotten any).

It's Great When the Seller Is Coasting

Technology can often produce large profit growth, even for non-tech businesses. A service business with burned-out owners (actually, they were well beyond burned out; they were fried) had a website that acted like a brochure. To order services, the customers had to call in, and we all know how that works—repeated phone tag.

Even if an order is left on voice mail, it must be confirmed. In any event, it takes an employee to process the order, and the customer must take time to make the calls, return calls, and talk about the order. The buyer noticed this during analysis and within two months had an online ordering system. It saved customer time and hassle, and it greatly increased his staff's productivity. It's not rocket science; it's observing, looking at things through the customers' eyes, and is equal to creating a "diamond in the rough." He doubled the business in two years.

In any event, for an ongoing business, the pool of targets is larger than if you are someone buying a first business (as most individual buyers avoid troubled companies like they avoid a toothache, because both are filled with pain). Look at the other eighteen reasons in this chapter for your prime motivation for making an acquisition, and use it to leverage your efforts.

Diversify Your Product Offerings

In chapter 1, there's a story about Fred's "picture-perfect" second acquisition. Let's investigate one aspect of it.

Almost every salesperson has left a client's business thinking, "If only we had the X and Y product line, I could sell it to him, save him money, and make more myself." Of course, it's tough to get those product lines, especially if you're starting from zero with the supplier.

Fred's company is an environmental testing laboratory. We came to find out there are different types of labs, and his original company dealt primarily with contaminants (groundwater, soil, etc.), so we call this a "dirty lab." Another type of lab, like his second acquisition, is what I call a "clean lab," testing drinking water (wells, reservoirs, municipal systems, etc.), food products, and similar products.

What we also learned is it's tough to do clean testing in a dirty lab, as the contaminants get in the air. To test water and food products, the lab needs to be scrubbed. Now he has a clean lab and a dirty lab, so he can offer each lab's customer base more services than before, and that's synergy.

The same applies to companies with a product. So why not buy a firm with complementary product lines and diversify what your people can sell? It doesn't have to be a huge company; it can be a small company that will have the full support of its vendor because you can plug the products into your customer base for almost instantaneous growth (of the new product lines).

The products don't have to be similar; the customer bases should use both types of products to leverage this idea. I remember one owner who sold packaging materials (boxes). He believed he could acquire a company that sold any kind of supplies to warehouses. What else do warehouses use? Paper, tape, janitorial supplies, racks, material handling equipment, and more. Don't limit yourself. Think creatively.

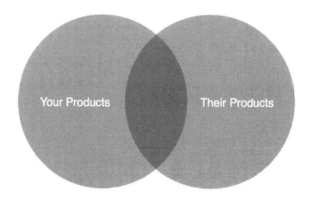

Easy Money

Easy money is the best kind.

How much does it cost to add a new product? What about expanding into a new market? To hire salespeople to generate new customers?

It can be a lot of money, so where do you get all that money? Will the bank lend you money to do these things? If so, how much and on what terms and conditions? And what are the chances of success?

I've presented a lot of questions in the previous two paragraphs, so how about some answers? (I know, another question.) You'll get all the money for organic growth by saving your profits or taking out a conventional bank loan.

But money for an acquisition is usually a lot easier to find. As we'll see in more detail later, banks really like acquisition loans. The bottom line is, if you tell your banker you're going to grow by 50 percent or more in the next year and need a loan for the growth, I'm guessing you'll be politely shown the door. At the very least, you'll be asked for detailed projections, an analysis showing the chances of success, and you'll be subject to intense scrutiny.

Now imagine you show them the profit and loss (P&L) and tax return for your target company, with more than enough historical annual flow to make the payments. A short synopsis of why the target is a fit, a brief overview of the integration plan, and a combined org chart may be everything else you'll need (and you'll need these anyway to make an acquisition).

This is easy money compared to just about any other type of growth funding.

Integration Is Easier

"People don't like change" is an old expression. What many people don't like is having their routines changed, especially without a reason or reward. Yes, there will be some change, and it will take time, but it's often easier than finding talent, integrating individuals, and changing the culture.

Create a Breath of Fresh Air

The sales manager at a recently acquired firm thanked me for getting the deal done and said the new buyer was a "breath of fresh air." The new owner, unlike the seller, listened to the employees' ideas, let them act on them, and was willing to take risks. Too often, employees get in a rut. They like the company and their jobs, but it gets to be routine. When the boss ignores them, they lose enthusiasm and leave.

A breath of fresh air is what you can inject when buying another business. Enthusiasm is hard to teach, but it's contagious. The excitement of an acquisition can fire up your team and the team of the acquired business with a new and rewarding challenge. Often, their company is being sold because the owner is retiring or burned out. In either event, that owner has probably been coasting while the employees are constantly having new ideas. Put two fired-up teams together, let them use their abilities, and you have 2+2 = 22.

The first positive here is you should have a larger management team, whether it's senior or junior people. This should give you a more diverse skill set or the ability to replace duplicate people with people who have other skill sets. Finally, there will be new ideas from their people regarding your operation and from your people regarding their operation.

This is what you are striving for with management and other employees as you create your breath of fresh air.

Daniel Pink, in his book *Drive*, quotes an owner talking about his employees: "They're not resources; they're partners." Here are my top three factors:

- Employees want to see their ideas at least considered, if not accepted.
- They want to feel a sense of accomplishment, understand their value, and be part of a winning team.
- Partners work toward a common goal.

Friendliness

The first assumption here is a win-win deal was structured. What you are offering to the seller is true value, whether it's a successful retirement, saving his sinking ship, or rescuing him from a catastrophic event (divorce, death, or disability).

When it's a win-win deal, you are on the same side, not battling each other. Synergies come together, people come together, and a happy seller may provide real value (now that she is freed from running a business).

Systems

There are three primary things here:

1. You get their systems, and they get yours, the best of the best.
2. With a larger company, you have the capacity to put in more and better systems (one reason being you may now have better people who can create systems).
3. After the transition, you should have time to do this.

Location, Location, Location

This is the old mantra for retail, and it applies to other industries also. There may be a location you want and can't get. It could be a retail location, and it could be, for manufacturers and distributors, a building near a distribution center, on a rail line, or close to suppliers. While this may not be a singular reason for making an acquisition, when combined with some of the other reasons, it may be your tipping point. More apropos for most companies is to expand geographically by buying a similar business (competitor) in another market (i.e., a new location).

Here's How It Works

One of my clients purchased a business in a different state, similar to his Seattle company. It gave him added volume and the opportunity for faster growth, and he could hire an industry friend to be the chief salesperson. The acquired firm had no sales team, as the owners, in their seventies, weren't active; they were coasting.

Make a Competitor Go Away

Some businesses have more than general industry competition; they have a specific competitor that stands in their way. It may be a fierce rival (along the lines of bitter sports rivals like the Steelers and Bengals or Yankees and Red Sox), or it may be there isn't a big enough market for either firm to break away from the other.

Acquire your competitor (or merge if you're friendly). This may make fast growth easier, cheaper, and more achievable. It may allow for faster moves into other markets or segments, using traditional growth strategies. This strategy ties in very well with the previous strategy of expanding geographically by acquisition. Keep in mind, if the rivalry is too bitter, there isn't much hope of a deal.

Real-Life Example
Here's a story about M&A among small businesses and the power of economies of scale. It's from my friend Ted Leverette at "Partner" On-Call Network, LLC.

One of my clients owned a profitable printing business. But it was not all it could be. Its owner was nervous because the customer pie wasn't growing. Worse, the slices were diminishing, thanks to new competition generated by the incursion of franchise print-shop start-ups. The owner was thinking about selling his company. I suggested he postpone selling until we could improve the company's competitive advantages.

My client was only running one shift. We acquired two competitors, each of whom served differing market segments, the kinds of customers we did not serve. Both of the acquisitions were earning a modest profit. Their owners wanted out because they, too, didn't want to cope with what was looking to be industry saturation.

We shut down the premises of both these acquisitions. We relocated some of their assets to our shop. We scheduled some of their employees on to our second and third shifts. We used some of the cash we generated from selling surplus equipment and the cost savings by elimination of overhead (rent and lots of other expenses) to pay down the financing we incurred to acquire the competitors. The company immediately increased its profit and improved its competitive advantages. And then the owner sold it for a lot more money than he would have gotten had he sold the company before doing what we did.

Overhead the Same, Volume Higher

Look at all the strategies preceding and following. Ninety percent or more of the time, you will add volume without adding (all) the corresponding overhead. This is often one of the prime motivators for acquiring. If you have forty employees and two staff accountants and the other firm has twenty-five employees and two staff accountants, there is a good chance you'll only need three staff accountants after the acquisition. Boom! One salary, tax, and benefit package goes to the bottom line. Or, as in Fred's story, he could hire an accountant versus a bookkeeper. The same can happen with rent, other staff, phone, Internet, advertising, and more.

Real-Life Story
A client bought one of his suppliers. It was a small business with a lot of inefficiencies. He moved the business into his space, replaced at least one production worker (my client had capacity), and coordinated marketing efforts with no increase in his marketing costs. In addition, think of all the other overhead he could eliminate, including telephone lines, accounting services, and utilities. He took a sleepy little company and turned almost all its gross profit into pure net profit.

Psychology
Employees want to be part of a winning team. They want to feel they're contributing to a winning effort. It's very much like sports; the more the team wins, the greater the number of fans it has.

I'm thinking of a young man I know who in his midtwenties. He took a while to figure out some things in life, is now steadily employed, and has been for the last few years (with the same company). He's proud of his job and his contribution and showed disdain when a new, younger employee (whom he called "the kid") flaunted the rules and wasn't dedicated. Let's be honest; some employees at this level don't care, but they're not the ones who are important anyway, like "the kid."

Now elevate this to the more experienced people, including the management team. In one company, there was some doubt about the general manager accepting new ownership. However, this doubt was unfounded, as he leaped at the chance to implement quality controls, better processes, and accountability.

As mentioned earlier, when you create a breath of fresh air, the employees will want to be part of it.

Risk Is a Lot Lower

John decided to grow his company into another market and did so by starting a new branch. Other than having vendor relationships, everything was new. But John couldn't manage the remote location as well as his home location (small businesses need "adult supervision"), and within a couple of years, he was in big trouble. This led to him having to divest his home location to pay the debts of his start-up.

Now, imagine John had acquired a company selling similar products (in the remote market). Given all the other eighteen reasons, it becomes evident his risk would have been greatly reduced.

Synergy

In an oversimplified example, you sell paper, and the company down the street sells envelopes. You sell to the same customer base. Wouldn't it make sense for one salesperson, not two, to call on each customer to sell paper and envelopes? The same holds true for delivery people, warehouse people, and accounting (one monthly invoice, not two).

These situations don't come up every day. Savvy owners are always on the lookout for them, though. It doesn't have to be as blatant an example as paper and envelopes. This is one reason my friend Fred jumped on his second acquisition, even though it was sooner than he preferred. He can now more easily market multiple services without much extra effort or cost. (I've used Fred's acquisitions numerous times because it's such a good example and it's fresh in my mind.)

Technologies

I remember talking with a gate agent for Delta Airlines immediately after they bought Northwest Airlines (also affectionately known as North Worst Airlines). I asked how the merger was going, and she made two comments. The first had to do with Delta's customer service strength, which Northwest did not have (as a frequent Northwest flyer, I agreed).

The second statement was about how Northwest had some of the best technology in the industry, and it would immediately upgrade Delta's technology.

Find a company with the ERP system you wish you had—or the automated processes or cloud access so all offices are "alive" all the time, or just about anything else to do with technology.

Vendor-Relationship Strategies

Diversifying vendors means accessing vendors you can't get on your own. Many have territories to protect their distributors and retailers. Acquiring one of their customers gets you in the door. Once in the door, you can make the most of the opportunity.

All of this assumes you're buying a company with different products than yours. This also works for buying a competitor (or similar business in another market) with the same product line. For retailers, this means buying a store that carries the same lines you carry. The result in either case is you will do higher volumes with your suppliers and qualify for greater (volume) discounts.

The Icing: The Top Three

Now here are the top three reasons to grow by acquisition.

Customers

"This would be a great business if it wasn't for those darn customers" was a semiserious comment someone made to me years ago. Of course, it's the annoying (bad) customers he was referring to. It's good customers we all want more of—customers who are loyal, steady, in good financial shape, growing, pay their bills on time, appreciate the value you offer, and consider you part of their team.

I mentioned earlier that acquiring a new product or service line you can sell to your customers is a good reason for an acquisition. The same holds true for selling your current offerings to a new group of customers. Often this can be done without any increase in your sales force (or sales forces if you consider the salespeople with the acquired firm).

An ideal situation is where there are some overlapping products, so there is some continuity and synergy to be achieved. The following figure shows this. Your salespeople now have an easy transition to discussing, and selling, their products, and their salespeople have an easy transition to discussing, and selling, your products.

In simple terms, if your primary motivation is acquiring a customer base, you are acquiring market share. You may have many other reasons (as in this chapter), but the bottom line is you are buying customers, and that means top-line growth.

Yes, We Can!

This is not about ego; it is about building an exit strategy to get a higher selling price. Buying another company, assimilating it into your operation, and showing the combined profits are greater than the two individual companies' profits demonstrate to potential buyers this can be done. It proves you have the team that can integrate one operation into another.

This integration could be their assimilating your firm into theirs, or it could be a signal that growing your business (or now a division of theirs) is possible by further acquisitions. A management team that can successfully integrate other firms without major disruption and with immediate efficiencies is a valued team. Too many big mergers and acquisitions fail. Up to 95 percent of public mergers do not live up to expectations. A savvy buyer will appreciate this talent and experience associated with past integrations.

Real-Life Story

Keith Jackson's firm bought a small business that manufactured a handful of proprietary products; the business was overly dependent on the seller, his products, and his manufacturing skills, and it was marginally profitable, meaning there were small profits after paying the owner a fair market salary for his work. Bottom line, it was a great deal for both sides.

This was Keith's second acquisition. Three years prior, he'd bought a decades-old manufacturing and distribution company.

The small manufacturing business was one of the suppliers for the distribution side of his company. He knew the product, its potential, its weaknesses, and how to sell more of it than the seller was selling. This acquisition was also part of his overall exit strategy, as it showed he could purchase a company, absorb it into his operation (profitably), and increase his rate of return on assets and sales.

For the seller, Keith was a lifesaver. Who else was going to buy a company so dependent on the owner's product-development skills and product knowledge? Surely not an individual wanting to own her own business. Not another company without any insight into the product and its markets. Plus, the seller got a consulting job with Keith to engineer the products he had invented and the products Keith's company had already made. Keith's insights and tips are at the end of chapter 4.

The Bigger You Are…the Better

The larger your business, the more it will sell for, all other things being equal. A $50 million (revenue) company with 10 percent EBITDA will sell for a higher multiple (of profit, EBITDA, free cash flow, or whatever metric you use) than a $25 million company with 10 percent EBITDA, which will sell for a higher multiple than a $15 million company, and so on.

There are generally accepted ranges for multiples of EBITDA, based on the range of the companies' revenue. However, too many small business owners see in the *Wall Street Journal* that a $300 million company in their industry sold for ten times EBITDA and assume their small business will also sell for ten times. That won't happen; there's more risk in smaller businesses than larger, so the desired return on investment is higher.

Here's an example

Companies with sales of $5–50 million historically have sold for four to seven times EBITDA, with those on the higher end selling for the higher end of the multiple range. Grow your $5 million company to $15 million, and your multiple may increase by one times EBITDA (from four to five, for example). Assuming 10 percent profit (and a four multiple), you can see the price go from $2 million to $7.5 million (10 percent profit at five times).

The fastest and safest way to grow from $5 to 15 million is by acquisition. Buy another firm in your industry—a supplier, customer, or unrelated company that provides diversification—to have an immediate revenue increase and a larger platform from which to grow organically. See more profit and a higher multiple when you exit.

> It's not bragging if you can do it.
> —Dizzy Dean (1934)

A lot of business owners talk about their company's potential or the growth that will occur if the buyer just "does some marketing." Of course, most of this is just talk. Business buyers of all types and sizes are a skeptical lot. When they hear too much about potential, they think the seller has tried every conceivable way to grow and can't.

So prove you can do it. Grow organically, and also go out and buy another company. Show you can integrate the people, processes, financial systems, customer service, and everything else into your operation. Private equity groups and large corporations make multiple acquisitions. If you can buy another firm and successfully assimilate it, you become more attractive to these buyers. They will assume you can do it again and your management team is capable. Strategic buyers and equity group buyers highly value management teams—it can even increase the multiple (compared to having the same size company that has not made acquisitions).

We've covered nineteen reasons why it makes sense to grow by acquisition. I realize most don't apply to your business. It's the few that do apply that are the reasons this strategy may make sense. Heck, your catalyst may be a reason not mentioned here. The point is this has worked for many companies, and you should always have your eyes open, looking for opportunities, as there are a lot of good reasons to do so.

At the same time, I must acknowledge there are pitfalls you need to avoid, but they can be avoided if handled correctly. How you handle the cultural integration makes a huge difference. Letting (most of) the employees, with both companies, know their jobs are safe is important, as with any acquisition. You will be taking on debt, but as mentioned, this debt comes with good things, like customers, good margins, cash flow, and other good things. If it makes sense to buy another company, these pitfalls are easily overcome.

Why They Made an Acquisition

Fred Barkman and Spectra Labs (www.spectra-lab.com) were the focus of some previous examples, and here are some insights from Fred.

Fred's primary reasons for buying additional companies are pretty basic—more products, geographic diversity, and more customers. With his third acquisition, it's also taking a competitor out of the market, plus getting some good equipment he'd be buying anyway.

Synergies have been important to Fred, and he's done well in this area. He's also a very charitable and caring person (we are in the same Rotary Club, and Rotary's tagline is "Service above self"). He likes the fact he's been able to make marginal companies profitable and give the employees more pay and better benefits.

In addition, his three acquisitions have

- allowed his first seller to realize a good retirement,
- given his second seller something for his retirement (it was a break-even business), and
- let his third seller go back to retirement (he had funded the lab for his son and was traveling from his home across the country to help out two weeks a year) and have his son move on to medical school.

Here are Fred's tips:

- Don't underestimate the amount of work and effort it will take to integrate the two companies.
- There are some things you won't know about the culture, the difference between your employees and theirs, and how issues are handled at the new company.

- It takes energy. You'll probably have to do new job descriptions, implement or modify management reports, and adjust processes and procedures.
- It takes time and money to see it through.
- Finally, if it's a competitor, know going in if there's any bad blood and if so how you will handle it.

CHAPTER 3

DO YOU WANT A DEAL OR AN EXPERIENCE?

L et's jump way ahead from the reasons to consider buying another business to getting the deal done. "Getting the Deal Done" is the title of one of my talks, an annual event I sponsor, and (likely) a future book. After all, isn't an acquisition all about getting the deal done?

The most important part is MRE—motivation, relationship, and education. Then come the reasons and rules that (for buyer and seller) will make it happen.

Motivation

If either party is not fully motivated, there will be no deal. Both parties must be fully motivated. A motivated seller is not someone who says he will sell for four times the fair price all in cash. A motivated buyer is not one who thinks a business is worth only what the assets are worth.

Let's start with the seller, as we'll assume you, the buyer, are motivated, at least for the right deal. A basic fact of buy-sell life is this:

> *The more catastrophic the event, the more urgency and motivation the seller has.*

The notorious three Ds lead the list: divorce, death, and disability (for now, let's only cover things happening to the owner, not the business; those come later).

Subsets of the three Ds include the following:

- The owner has a health scare.
- The owner's spouse has a health issue.
- One of the owner's friends has a heart attack, is diagnosed with cancer, or, heaven forbid, dies.

But most deals don't happen because of one of the three Ds, although the subset is a viable motivational alternative. Most happen because of one of the following:

Burnout

Management- and executive-level people in the United States change jobs (voluntarily or forced) every three to five years. Business owners are people too; sometimes they get bored, have other ideas, or need a refreshing change. It happens.

Why It's True

At the time of this book's publishing, I have led twelve International Rotary projects, "Improving Education through Technology." Nine of the twelve have been in the Caribbean country of Antigua and Barbuda. Working with the Bellevue, Washington, school district's technology department, we travel with fourteen high-school tech students, install computer labs and Wi-Fi networks, and contract out training for the teachers on how to teach more effectively by using technology (very important in this developing country).

Our project is dependent on the lead teacher, Jeff Mason, and me. We both put in countless hours on this, and while we find it tremendously rewarding, it can lead to burnout. I get to the point where I don't want to go near the Rotary grant website to fill out forms.

I get burned out primarily because the project is so dependent on the two of us—just like a small business where the owner gets sick of doing what she's been doing. Unlike many businesses, even if we wanted to delegate more, it's tough to do.

Retirement

If the owner is eighty or older, there's a 90 percent chance he will die at his desk. One of my client's top customers is in his late eighties, and the last I heard, the owner, who recently bought out his younger minority partner, says he plans to live forever and run the business as long as he's alive. Another owner, eighty-eight at the time I write this, finally feels his fifty-one-year-old son is mature enough to buy and run the business. However, he doesn't plan to leave; he'll still come in every day.

But many owners, or their spouses, want to retire and relax. A big factor is how long they've been in business. Age fifty-seven with twenty-eight years in is just as motivating as sixty-seven with fifteen years of ownership.

Dispute

A partnership or family dispute, it really doesn't matter. A dispute means motivation.

Real-Life Story

I was referred to a manufacturing business that's growing and has decent margins and two owners who have been together for too long. One wants out; the other says he wants to work for two more years because the pipeline is full.

Both call me to tell me how unreasonable his partner is. The one who wants to stay says he'll only sell for a price well above what the valuation says it's worth, but he won't pay his partner as much as the valuation says. The other partner won't take a discount from the valuation. Yikes! I tell them I can't help them.

Business Outgrows the Owner

I see multiple occurrences of this every year. The business gets to a size where it's no fun for the product-oriented owner. She's sick of managing people, processes, and money and wants to go back to when she could work "in" not "on" the business.

Entrepreneur Owner

Boredom sets in earlier than usual in this case. Entrepreneurs have a constant flow of ideas. For example, I spoke with a guy in his late thirties. He wanted to sell his business, which was his seventh start-up; the reason was he had an idea for another business. This is where your management experience and leadership can capitalize on a situation.

Life Happens

Whether it's bad luck or it's a bad personal decision, life happens.

- The seller had a special-needs son, and both her parents went into a nursing home the same weekend and died two months later, within a week or so of each other. The business had become an afterthought.
- Another seller leveraged all his assets to the maximum and invested in commercial real estate in 2007. We know what happened in 2008. The bank forced him to sell the business to pay down his real-estate debt.

Simply put, if something affects the owner, it's a good cause of motivation.

However, what if something affects the business? This may be an opportunity for you, as another business can take over and absorb an operation with lower overall costs, which is something a financial buyer can't do.

That said, in my twenty-plus years in the buy-sell field, I've only worked on four deals where a distressed company was involved. In all but one case, it was operator error (i.e., a bad business decision). The other case was a lack of succession plan, as after the founder/owner died, the spouse reaped the cash flow until the lack of adult supervision eliminated the cash flow, and it had to be sold for whatever they could get (lucky buyer, who did great).

In all cases, whether I represented the buyer or seller, it was obvious what needed to be done; the buyer did it, the business turned around, and did great.

As stated, as an existing business owner, you have options financial buyers don't have. You can look at marginal profit, breakeven, and even losing money. As per chapter two, consolidating them into your operation will make that business a profitable division.

Relationship

One of my favorite rules regarding buy-sell deals is as follows:

Cash is king (and so is cash flow). But the queen is relationships, and like in chess, the queen is the most powerful piece in the game. It's a relationship game, and don't forget it; nobody buys from or sells to someone they don't like.

The phrase "I would never buy (a business) from or sell to somebody I don't like" came from a client who started a company. We sold it to a competitor and then went out and bought two businesses. Ever since he put it so succinctly, I have used this phrase to stress the importance of relationships to audiences and clients.

So what does this really mean? It means if you meet a seller (or, if you're selling, a buyer), and at your first meeting, you spend two hours together, talk about the business for fifteen minutes, and then you have a lot in common. It could be business in general, sports, kids, fishing, management philosophy, or just about any other subject.

The Right Way

I was coaching one of our "Partner" On-Call Network franchisees on building relationships, as he was having a tough time getting to know people and building relationships. We talked as he drove to his meeting and again immediately after.

I prepped him to observe things in the other person's office and find commonality, and if there wasn't any commonality, then simply ask about things he saw.

Our postmeeting conversation had a very happy camper. He found two common areas as I recall. They were Little League and boating. He started the conversation with one of those and moved on to the other, and his meeting, for which the person had allocated a strict thirty minutes, went on for ninety minutes.

The Wrong Way

One of my clients was a marketing person. Not the typical outgoing marketing person but an expert in technical marketing (online primarily). Not only that, but he also told me he didn't buy into "all the relationship stuff."

The matter reached a head when he called me one day to complain about all the sellers who really didn't want to sell. I looked at his file and told him it was three times the size of any other buyer client's file (his leads to companies).

Then I told him about a conversation I had had with an owner a couple of days prior. The owner told me he wanted to sell his business, just not to this buyer.

You see, this buyer had a practice of starting the meeting off by going directly to "Show me your financial statements and tax returns, and let me drill deep on what makes this company tick (we'll call it the secret sauce)." Of course, owners were skittish about sharing this with someone they just met. And it's a big reason his meetings lasted about twenty minutes, not a couple of hours.

The more time you spend getting to know somebody, the faster the process will move.

How and Why It Works
There were four offers on the business (a very nice value-add distributor). My client's offer was $250,000 less than the highest offer (on a $4 million deal). He got the deal because of the relationship, and the seller didn't even ask him to match the highest offer, only to raise his price by $100,000. Relationship building got him a deal and saved him $150,000.

Education
Once you find a motivated seller and build a relationship, it's time for education. Here are some of the factors both sides need to understand.

- It's a process of give and take. Lines in the sand rarely work. Deals happen when both sides are equally unhappy (and often this is shown by both proclaiming all they've done is give while the other party hasn't given much).
- The buy-sell process itself is one of analysis, deal structure, and then due diligence (by both sides). Diligence proves what's been shared earlier and is not a time for surprises; it's a time for confirmation.
- Buyer and seller remorse will manifest itself; that's a given. So be prepared for it. It's also known as deal fatigue as things drag on.
- There are ranges of value for different-size businesses, and it's rare the price will fall outside that range (more on valuation later).

Real-Life Story

I remember sitting in a coffee shop with a buyer and seller. They were struggling with the deal, moving forward, and what to do next. I explained to the buyer, "A good business with an owner you like doesn't come along very often, so do what you can do to get the deal done." I told the seller, "A qualified buyer with money is not the easiest person to find, so do what you can do to get the deal done." They verbally came to an agreement within fifteen minutes.

After the other party left, my client said to me, "You earned your whole fee in this meeting. Thank you."

- Industry buyers know where the skeletons are, under what rugs the secrets are kept, and exactly what to ask (about key metrics and indicators). Letting a seller know this, subtly, early in the process helps.
- It's all about the free cash flow, the money left after paying all management salaries (including the owner's), capital expenditures, and operating interest.
- As we've seen, there are some generally accepted ranges of value (more on this later) for certain sized companies and certain industries. The deal will be in this range, given an intelligent buyer and seller, 95 percent of the time.
- It's more than the numbers. The nonfinancial factors are as or sometimes even more important than the numbers.
- It will take time. It will take you a minimum of six to twelve months from the start of the search and at least 90–120 days once you first meet a seller.

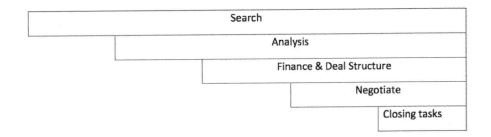

Here's a list of additional tips.

- Look at a variety of companies so you have choices. Being able to compare and contrast is very important. Searching for a business is like sales; it's the same as your business prospecting for customers. Have a proven search plan and implement it properly.
- Know your criteria, which means don't go into it thinking, "I'll know it when I see it." Define the must-have features and the want-to-have features.
- Take action when you see where you can add value. Pay more than you might normally pay if you absolutely, positively know how you can increase sales, reduce costs, or otherwise add value.
- Don't fall in love with the product. Fall in love with the business model and its value proposition. This means you want a business with a defensible competitive advantage. Know how you will integrate the business and exploit its competitive advantage. As Warren Buffett says, "The key to investing is not assessing how much an industry is going to affect society, or how much it will grow, but rather determining the competitive advantage of any given company and, above all, the durability of that advantage.[1]
- Don't get analysis paralysis (the bigger the spreadsheet, the less chance of a deal happening). This especially applies to finance and engineer types (as well as those not sure they want to make an acquisition).
- Realize there are no perfect businesses and no perfect deals. Get over it if you think you'll find a business without flaws. Get over it even more if you think there's a perfect deal. Deals happen

when both sides are equally unhappy. I'm not saying overpay, but paying at the high end of the fair price range and growing the company, consolidating costs, or leveraging it with your existing customers means more than worrying too much about price.

- Understand terms and conditions are often more important than price. This is where seller motivations come into play. An offer in the fair price range will often tell you if price, cash at closing, long-term involvement, or getting out ASAP are what negotiations will concentrate on.

- Be very careful if there are dependencies in the business. As mentioned, the first place to look is at the owner. How dependent is the business on him or her? There can also be dependencies involving customers, vendors, key employees, technology, or other things.

- Make sure the seller understands the bank and you will be "nosy" these days, very nosy. Banks are asking due-diligence questions buyers didn't ask before the 2008 recession. And you will ask even more questions than the bank.

- Don't be a "defensive" buyer. There is risk; you will take some, and so will the seller.

- Understand the administrivia near closing will drive you nuts but must be done. So deal with it!

- Make your starting benchmark for financing 50 percent of profit to acquisition debt (a 2:1 debt coverage ratio). The larger the deal, the more you can move to a 1.5:1 ratio (there are only very few, if any, circumstances where you will want to go to the bank's minimum of 1.25:1). A good business-acquisition banker won't let you go below about 1.5:1. As a grow-by-acquisition buyer, you have an advantage with banks. Many banks will look at the combined entities' cash flow for their ratios, which is why they'll often finance a break-even business.

You will make a leap of faith. Do it right, and that leap is off a chair, not the roof. Keep in mind the only thing worse than no deal is a bad deal. Be patient, and don't get "buyer fever." You have a good business, which is why you're thinking of an acquisition, so the worst that can happen is you are left with a good business, right?

Why They Made an Acquisition

Eric Johnson founded and has owned AFTS (www.afts.com) for over forty years. AFTS provides statement and mailing services (clients are utilities and other organizations where it's not mass mailing or it's confidential), collection services for seller-financed real-estate deals, and other payment processing between private parties.

Eric estimates they have made over fifteen acquisitions, many of them picking up a portfolio from a bank that got out of the payment-processing business, along with at least six true company acquisitions where he got the people, customers, office space, or geographic expansion.

He likes the dynamic of doing something different, as it gives him self-enjoyment. He also said it's good for the ego as the seller is saying he or she trusts you with the business, to do a better job than he or she did. Plus, it's easier than beating the streets for more customers.

Eric's tips to you are the following:

- Have empathy. Put yourself in their shoes; think like them.
- As part of the empathy, ask yourself if you'd take the deal you're offering them.
- Watch the numbers. Analyze the historical, make projections, and use the numbers, not just your gut feeling.
- Don't get overconfident (i.e., buyer fever).
- Do it because it makes sense, not just because you want to do it.
- Finally, get help from people very experienced in deals. They will be impartial without the emotion. It may be costly, but it's well worth it.

CHAPTER 4

WINGING IT IS FOR ROOKIES: TRUST THE PROCESS

S o any business that adds revenue is a candidate? Really?

Have a Plan and Follow It

It's important to define what you want before starting to search, even more important than when a corporate refugee decides to buy a business because you have not only a business model to fit it into but also a business to run.

It's a lot more than the type of business. Yes, as a widget distributor, you know it will probably be related to the widget industry, but there's a lot more to think about. In fact, it may not be in the widget industry but may offer many other advantages. Here are seven things to think about.

1. What can you absorb safely? Most companies buy smaller or similar-sized firms. I can only think of one client who bought a much larger company (it was three times the size), and that was part of his plan given some of the employees he had brought on board. Remember, you must also integrate employees, not just sales and customers.

2. Your available cash and the target's profitability determine the price or at least the bulk of it. As we'll see later, businesses in certain size ranges have ranges of value that aren't deviated from

(too often). You aren't going to get "a steal" unless the business is a loser and you are the knight in shining armor riding to the rescue; you're still buying a loser and its related culture.

3. Local location within the metropolitan area. I live in the Seattle area. It's a large geographic area with hills, bridges, and over-crowded freeways. A business in the south suburbs buying a company in the north suburbs will lose many employees if they consolidate to either location, or employees may experience frustration when key people (perhaps you) must travel between sites.

Examples

A client owns a 125-employee manufacturing business and knew they must move from Seattle proper. Move south and they lose 50 percent of their employees. Move north and they lose up to 20 percent of their employees.

Another company makes and delivers a lightweight but bulky product (not too many can fit on a truck, as most of what is being transported is air). Their geographic area is limited, as they have a price-sensitive product, and too much time sitting in traffic kills the margins. These same things apply when you consider an acquisition.

4. Replacement skills—what duties of the seller do you need to replace? Or do you keep the seller on as an employee? It's fifty-fifty if the seller will be a good employee as the following examples demonstrate. If he doesn't stay on, who does his job as you already have responsibilities?

Should the Seller Stay or Go?

Bob bought a company that had outgrown the owner/seller. The seller stayed on in sales and once freed from management went out and did a fantastic job. He's a salesman, not a manager.

Tom's situation was similar in that the company had outgrown the capabilities of the two owners. In this case, he needed the sellers to stay on (it wasn't an option), and even though everything was warm and fuzzy up to and through closing, it changed quickly. One of the sellers, the one in charge of sales, couldn't handle working for someone else. After years of being his own boss, it just didn't sit right and caused a major disruption to the business.

This is an important area. Be sure you know what you need and what you're getting.

5. Who do you need? Probably just about everybody, and the good news is they want to stay. Sure, there may be some people who will be redundant, but when it comes to the skilled people, that's what you want, isn't it? As one buyer said to his seller when the seller didn't want to let him meet the key employees prior to closing (after the purchase and sale agreement was signed), "You may think I'm buying your business, but I'm really buying your people."

6. The following stool shows everybody's thoughts and feelings. The buyer wants the employees, the seller wants the employees to keep their jobs, and the employees want to keep their jobs. Yet all think one of the other parties feels different.

7. The sales system—is it like yours? Is the technology the same (salesforce versus other systems, etc.)? Do they have internal or external salespeople? This is something you need to think about early in the process, as it's tough to get salespeople to make

drastic changes. Ask yourself, what do I need? Are you looking for technology, people, customers, products, sales volume, or something else?

Examples

- Keith bought product lines (some he distributed, and some he just wanted).
- Bob bought customers and the people to service them.
- Fred, mentioned earlier, bought a full package.
- Eric bought volume.
- Jim's motivation was also more volume via more products.
- Mark bought opportunity by buying what he considered an underperforming business (and he got a lot of volume).

Nine Steps to Success

You have a process for selling and delivering your product or service, and I'm sure you have your employees follow that process. So have a process to locate, analyze, and structure a deal. Here's my nine-step process, the same process outlined in my other books, *Buying a Business that Makes You Rich* and *If They Can Sell Pet Rocks, Why Can't You Sell Your Business (For What You Want)?* It's a process I've used with hundreds of business-buyer clients.

1. Preparation, search, and screening
2. Financing
3. Analysis
4. Valuation and pricing
5. Deal making
6. Negotiation
7. Due diligence
8. Transition planning
9. Closing

Preparation

Preparation means defining as many criteria as you can up front and be-ing as wide as you possibly can be with those criteria. The previous seven factors are a good starting point for your preparation. You need to know exactly what you're looking for in a target company.

Ninety-four percent of privately held business have sales under $10 million. That means your chances of buying a smaller company are much greater than your chances of buying the largest business you can afford. This also means lower financial risk and a smaller chance of tran-sition shock.

Define the basics of a desired acquisition, like geographic area, size range, acceptable profit range, and industry. Does it do exactly what you do? Is it a customer, a vendor, or something unrelated to your business?

Then move into the softer criteria:

- What strengths do you want the management team and employ-ees to have?
- What kind of customers should the target firm have?
- Will the seller be expected to stay on, or will she leave ASAP?

The more you prepare before searching, the better results you will have.

Search and Screening

Your salespeople may be great at formulating win-win offers for your clients and fantastic at closing the sale. However, as important as those skills are, they are useless if the salespeople can't get in front of potential customers, that is, they have lousy prospecting skills. The same is true when searching for a company to acquire. Deal structure and expertise are useless if you don't find a company. A solid, proven search system is the key.

In my book *If They Can Sell Pet Rocks, Why Can't You Sell Your Business (For What You Want)?* I show business owners how to do what homeowners do when selling their houses—spiff it up and make it look good underneath the surface so it passes inspection (known as due diligence in buy-sell transactions). You know that's not easy, and so the chances are good your acquisition candidate will not have done this work (the *Wall Street Journal* reported only 10 percent of companies are prepared to sell for maximum value). If you find a prepared business, great; if not, perhaps that means you can add value, and that's opportunity.

In simple terms, finding a company to acquire that meets your criteria means you (pick your favorite cliché) beat the bushes, pound the streets, or turn over every rock to see if there is a motivated seller to be found. Often, the seller is scared, scared to death in some cases, that somebody (anybody) will find out the business may be for sale. That fear is legitimate. Employees get scared if they perceive big change, customers may start looking elsewhere, competitors will use it against them, and vendors may put them on COD.

So what's the market in the late 2010 decade? In my opinion, there's a normal number of buyers for small- to midsized business and a ton of buyers for middle-market companies (a lot of money chasing not enough deals). The pool of sellers is growing, as shown by the following statistics.

- Seventy percent of medium-sized companies will sell in the next decade, with an estimated $10 trillion of value.
- Two-thirds of companies with sales of $5–50 million will change hands in the next ten years.
- Sixty-five to seventy-five percent of small US companies, some ten million, will likely hang up a For Sale sign in the next ten years.

The above statistics come from the following:

- *The Wall Street Journal,* 2008
- *PricewaterhouseCoopers,* 2011
- *Inc.* magazine, 2015

So why the constant number of companies and "in the next ten years"?

- Sixty-six percent of businesses with employees are owned by baby boomers—Axial, 2015
- Sixty percent of business owners delayed their exit by at least two years due to the Great Recession—SunTrust Bank, 2010

To clarify, not all owners delaying their exit wanted to sell when the Great Recession hit. For many it took a few years to get back to where they were. And guess what? We've had a pretty good run from 2011 to 2018, and exiting can take a back seat when times are good. Or, "Recession, what recession?" That said, in 2016, I started saying how I've never seen so many construction-related businesses for sale as there have been currently (contractors, suppliers, etc.). Contractors vividly remember the last down cycle.

Real-Life Story

James was selling his small business to a larger competitor. Against my advice, he told his two key employees he was selling (before he had a deal). Within thirty days, both gave their notice, although one ended up staying.

An owner told me that he shared with a supplier that he was "thinking" of selling. The vendor put him on COD. When I shared that when speaking to a group of accountants, a lady in the back squirmed in her seat with her hand in the air. (I thought I'd missed the time for the break.) She wanted to tell me that her firm sold through distributors, and if they knew one was selling, their policy was also to put them on COD.

This points out that finding a business is hard work. It takes focus. It's not something you (or your staff or your acquisition advisor) do sporadically or haphazardly. Finding a company is like a sales effort. You must work your (prospecting) system consistently and constantly. This is tough while running a business. Assign tasks just like you would with any growth effort, monitor it, and track activities and results, as we'll see in more detail later.

To summarize, the following are some tips for searching for a business:

- Approach it the same way you approach any sales or marketing function.
- There has to be a plan; you (and your team) have to follow the plan, paying attention to the details.
- Your goal is to get in front of sellers in situations where you are the only buyer talking to them.
- It takes time, hard work, and smart work.
- You'll kick a lot of tires, but it'll be well worth it when you find the right match.

Screening

The most important part of the screening process is screening the individual (or individuals) selling the business. While at some point you will do a credit check and related background research, the first step is to find out if you are compatible with the seller.

You will be working with the seller for months (or years) during transition or if she becomes employed by your firm, but also think about it from this perspective: the seller has relationships with customers, vendors, and employees. If she gets along with them and you don't get along with her, or your styles are completely different, then how are you going to relate to the customers, vendors, and employees? That creates a culture clash, the issue that derails or at the very least disrupts large corporate mergers.

As mentioned, this means your first job when you meet a seller is to build some rapport. Find out if your styles and personalities are compatible. Not only can this make or break a deal, but it can also make or break the postdeal success.

Our initial preparation defined acquisition criteria including the basic search criteria of location, size, and type of business. You don't need to do too much more in this area, as the objective is to cast a wide net, filtering out those that don't meet your deeper criteria. Some of the criteria at the next level include the following:

- Cash flow or profit—do you need to buy a profitable company? Is it worth considering companies that are breaking even or losing money if you can absorb them and eliminate their overhead? Have an acceptable range and use it when screening companies. But don't eliminate companies too early as, unfortunately, many owners don't know their exact profit situation, and some, to protect themselves, won't give you an accurate number too soon in the discussions.
- What type of ownership structure are you willing to accept? In other words, are you looking for a pure acquisition, or would a merger work (especially with you retaining majority interest and control)?
- What type of management team and key employees are you looking for? For example, if your company is great at operations and your weakest area is sales, you may want to buy a firm with a strong sales department. Or maybe you just want added volume or line workers. Know what your preferences are going in.

Don't be afraid to ask the seller thought-provoking questions like the following:

- "What do you do on a daily, weekly, and monthly basis?"
- "What skills does the person taking over your role need to possess?"
- "What are the barriers to entry in your niche?"
- "How do you attract customers (relationship or marketing—there's a big difference)?"

Your objective is to eliminate candidates, for legitimate reasons, as soon as possible. And while you're planning, think about the answers you will give to questions you get from the seller. The right answer could solidify your deal. The wrong answer could kill it, and who knows how long it will take to find another qualified company? You don't want to divulge too much about your business too soon. Confidentiality is a two-way street.

Financing

Financing is the key to getting a deal done. No money means no deal. Without knowing your size, structure, or cash position, I offer four basic guidelines:

1. Cash talks, and the more cash a seller gets at closing, the more receptive he will be.

2. Providing equity in the acquired firm (also known as rollover equity) can have advantages. It will require a lower cash outlay lower debt (which your bank will like), and it will keep the seller onboard for years, if that's what you want. But don't ignore danger signs, including those indicating the seller and you will not work well together or those suggesting the seller may not gracefully relinquish decision making. (SBA bank loans require you to buy 100 percent of the company.)

3. Bank loans are readily available for acquisitions (keep in mind this is for profitable and fairly priced companies, not for losers/turnarounds), and as of this writing, the limit on Small Business Administration (SBA) guaranteed loans is $5 million. SBA guaranteed loans generally carry a longer term than a conventional loan—ten years; they are cash-flow lenders and require less cash down but have higher fees and usually higher interest rates.

4. Look for the cash flow or assets of the business to help pay for the business. This is creative financing. Every deal is different, and often, there are ways to get cash out of the business at closing or just after.

When it comes to bank loans, banks don't preapprove people, as they do mortgages. Even though some buyers, brokers, and sellers say they are preapproved, they really aren't. There is just no such thing because it depends on the business *and* the buyer. A bank may say a buyer is qualified for a loan up to a certain amount, but this is nowhere close to any kind of approval.

My strong advice is to get bankers involved sooner rather than later (you have a bank, so use it); however, if they aren't specialists on business-acquisition loans, you need to find bankers who are experts. I'll cover financing in detail later.

Real-Life Story

Robb bought a business where the seller loved assets. He loved seeing racks full of inventory. In his first year, Robb sold off $200,000 of inventory that he did not replace. Instead, he managed inventory better. That inventory turned into cash on his balance sheet and in his bank account.

FYI, most deals (not microdeals) should and do include average working capital.

Analysis

Analysis is the next step, although at this point, all the remaining steps in the process become intermingled, as we'll see. Unfortunately, this step is where many deals unnecessarily lose momentum. Too often, the buyer wants too much information too soon, and it spooks the seller. Remember, you may have just met the seller—it's premature to ask her to share her business secrets with you.

I advise a stepped approach. It starts with taking a look at the financial statements and working with the seller to "recast" or adjust them so you can see the true profit picture of the business. By this, I mean, you want to know what the bottom line would be if the business tried to show as much profit as possible instead of paying as little tax as possible. This means looking for those "lifestyle" expenses that many business owners run through their company. It also means adjusting the depreciation to allow for anticipated capital expenditures and looking for expenses that will disappear or will have to be added when you are the owner (although you shouldn't pay for the value you bring to the business).

At the same time, ask some big-picture questions about all the nonfinancial aspects of the business. For example (there are all-encompassing questions for all categories in the appendices), the following are some of the questions we ask about the technology side of the business:

- Is your technology up to date?
- Are all subscriptions current?
- Are there any virus or security issues?
- Does any hardware or software need upgrading (is the hardware less than three years old)?

If no, please explain the situation and the estimated cost.

A no answer lets you probe and lets you feel comfortable until it is time to delve deeper. As we ask these questions, we let the seller know we will accept his answers, base a deal on those answers, and then prove what he told us during due diligence. We'd prefer to hear any bad news now instead of being surprised in due diligence, which is a time for confirmation, not discovery.

These technology questions are one small section in my initial disclosure form. If you'd like a copy, please e-mail me at john@johnmartinka.com. This form was designed to uncover big red flags early and get them on the table for review.

Value and Pricing

Valuation is covered in chapter 8, so let me just comment on value versus price. Value is based on formulas and methodologies. Value takes into account both the financial and the nonfinancial factors. Price is the perceived value agreed upon by the buyer and the seller. The price can be, and often is, different from the value because value is theoretical and price is real world.

How the price is paid, as previously mentioned, affects price (not value). Motivation and need affect price (not value). A seller who needs a certain amount of cash at closing may sell for a lower overall price. A buyer with less cash or who really needs to fill a gap in her business (via this acquisition) may pay more. Always seek counsel from a transaction tax expert on this subject.

That said, there is a strong correlation between value and price. No matter what someone's feelings, a price has to be supported by a valuation, especially if there's a bank involved in the deal.

Value and Price Must Be Close

Many years ago, my associate Ted Leverette and I did valuations for banks. There was a special situation where the bank was required to get two valuations. The buyer and seller had agreed on the price, the bank was willing to make the loan, and we couldn't come close to the price, no matter how we looked at it. Their price was almost 25 percent more than our value. (Like in real estate, often an appraiser will agree with the market price if his valuation is close. He'll figure the market is the ultimate determining factor. In our case, we couldn't do this, as the cash flow simply didn't support the price based on the industry and risk factors.)

The banker was furious. He told me the other appraiser "simply rubber-stamped the price." Not comforting if you're a shareholder of that bank, is it? Needless to say, we never did another valuation for that bank or banker.

Deal-Making and Negotiation

Later, I'll give a detailed process that works great, whether the seller is working with an investment banker, business broker, on her own, or with her CPA and attorney. It gets you to the deal components, which are common to all deals: price, terms, and conditions. Price and terms are pretty self-explanatory and covered by the previous process, the financial information, and nonfinancial questions. Conditions vary from deal to deal. Conditions could include (but are not limited to) the following:

- Employment contracts with key employees
- Environmental reports
- Due-diligence issues specific to the company
- Lease assignment with extension or a new lease
- Financing
- Employees signing noncompete and nonsolicitation agreements
- Vendor agreements
- Customer contract assignments

As you get ready to formulate a deal structure that will lead to an offer, here are three things you should at least consider doing:

1. Consult someone in the valuation field and perhaps get a limited opinion of value.
2. Start talking to bankers. Even if you don't plan to use a bank to help finance the deal, I recommend you talk to some. They look at companies and deals differently than entrepreneurs do; they are in business to get paid back.
3. Work with your acquisition advisor and your management team to formulate your strategy so this doesn't distract from your day-to-day operations, and decide how much cash you plan to invest.

As mentioned, some banks love acquisition loans and some don't understand them. Your bank may be great to work with, but if it doesn't have a history and culture of liking acquisition loans, you won't get very far. Do some research to find out which banks understand and like these loans.

Some banks only care about assets (collateral), some care primarily about cash flow (as we'll see, SBA loans are "cash-flow" loans), and many are in the middle, meaning they want some of both. Play the field, as you never know what will happen, and the bank's approach to acquisition loans is often a key component to getting a loan and a deal.

Real-Life Story

The owner of two very successful businesses with a long entrepreneurial track record was purchasing another, unrelated business. He worked closely with one large bank while keeping others in the wings. The loan officer, credit manager, and committee liked the deal, so it went to HQ for final approval. As I understand it, it passed muster at the first three levels, and then the final decision-maker at the corporate HQ rejected the loan, saying, "I never liked that industry."

This caused a lot of broken hearts (buyer, banker, and seller). It was then on to another bank. The community bank that made the deal looked at the buyer's history of being an entrepreneur as much as anything ("character" is the term used) to make the loan.

We are talking about relationship-based deals here. If the negotiations get contentious or the attorneys get involved in negotiating deal points (not legal points), it can be tough to get the deal back on track. That's why it is often beneficial for both sides to have an intermediary on their team. The intermediary can wear the "black hat," be the bad guy (or gal), have the knowledge and experience to mitigate potential problems, and can disarm minor issues that the inexperienced person might magnify out of proportion. I've been involved in many behind-the-scenes discussions that keep the deal on track without letting the buyer's or seller's emotions take center stage.

One final word on this subject—the deal has to work for you; it also has to work for the seller. Emotions get in the way, so don't get unrealistic buyer fever. As a buyer, hope the seller likes you so much he or she gives you an asking price that is more than fair (which does happen fairly often).

Due Diligence

As with valuation, volumes have been written on due diligence. A master due-diligence list with some standard due-diligence topics and questions is provided in the appendix. Once both parties have agreed to a deal structure, signed a nonbinding letter of intent (LOI), and the purchase and sale agreement are being drafted, it is time for due diligence. Whether on the buy or sell side of the table, you should expect a lot of questions.

Due diligence is the process of proving what you've been told (the facts on which you based the offer). During the process, you may also uncover some risks that may cause you to change or kill the deal, or you may uncover opportunities you didn't know about (meaning "let's get it done sooner versus later").

A lot of buyers think, "Shouldn't I be performing due diligence before I make an offer?" As per the above process, the answer is no, and here's the main reason. Take some time to consider it from the seller's perspective. If you were the seller, and you will be someday, would you let a buyer talk to your employees, customers, vendors, or landlord before you had a deal in place? Would you want a buyer reviewing your books, seeing your business plan, and getting other secrets and strategies from you? This is why you tell the seller, "I will base my offer on this early information and will prove it during due diligence. So please tell me about any things that might concern me now, as I don't want to be surprised and have to renegotiate the deal later."

So what exactly is due diligence? In simple terms, it is investigating all the details and intricacies of a business to verify the business is what you thought it was (or better than you thought). You will break down the financial statements, prepare a budget, construct a pro forma balance sheet, and do a month-by-month cash-flow projection. On the nonfinancial side, you will discreetly interview customers (not telling them you are buying the company), talk to the management team and key employees, work with the landlord on your lease, interview vendors, and if there are any contracts, get approval to transfer them to you. In addition, you will update or prepare a business plan (for yourself and the bank).

Transition Planning

Too often so much emphasis is put on getting the deal closed that the day after closing, the buyer shows up, and it's "Now what?" Integrating the acquired business with your business the right way will be covered later, so I won't elaborate here. There's a detailed example of a transition plan in chapter 10.

Process Wrap-up

Buying a business or another business is not for everybody. There are serious risks involved, and that is why the rate of return is much higher than on other investments (like mutual funds, publicly traded stocks, bonds, etc.). However, if you want to grow sooner rather than later or position yourself for an eventual sale, buying another business is faster, cheaper, safer, and easier to finance than starting a new division, opening a branch in another city, or increasing your sales and marketing efforts to grow organically.

If you desire any of the goals associated with growth by acquisition, you owe it to yourself to investigate it. Follow a proven plan, and pay attention to the details. Put together a team, including your attorney, accountant, acquisition advisor, and banker. Make sure all have experience in transactions of the type you are targeting. Keep in mind that preparation and planning make the process go faster and smoother. As the late Lionel Haines (a noted author of many books on the buying and selling of businesses) said, "You must act like a hunter, not a trapper." You have to get out there and actively search for businesses, as you would prospect for new customers. This is not a passive sport.

Once you find a good candidate, don't create your own speed bumps or roadblocks. There are enough already out there! There is risk involved, and if you feel your skills balance the risks of the business you are considering, then delve in and find out what makes that company tick. In other words, why is it profitable or unprofitable? Some of the best deals are when a money-losing company is "saved" by someone in the industry who can make money on the same sales volume (or, as a better manager, do little things that make a big difference). When growing by acquisition, take the time to look at almost all businesses because you have different criteria than a pure financial buyer (who needs a salary, profit, etc.).

Why They Made an Acquisition

Keith Jackson with Industrial Revolution (www.industrialrev.com), also the subject of some examples, has made three or four additional acquisitions, mostly to get additional products.

When asked why, he replied, "It's for growth—to supplement organic growth with new companies and products to create a larger platform for more growth including cross marketing." He also likes the process because it's "big-picture work." It's more interesting to him than dealing with customer problems, employee issues, etc. Also, he has the potential to change the company (both companies).

One of his acquisitions didn't do as well as planned and hoped for. The industry had peaked, and what he got wasn't the same as the historical market. In addition, and this is important, as I've mentioned it before, the seller was to remain onboard but didn't handle not being in control very well.

Keith advises others to realize there are always red flags (or, as I like to say, there are no perfect businesses or perfect deals), just know how many red flags are too many. Be prepared to walk away from deals, as he has, if you don't feel you'll have the bandwidth to deal with the process, you sense a lack of enthusiasm, or there are other issues, often people.

However, he also states you should realize you can make a big difference to your firm, the seller, and the employees.

CHAPTER 5

FINDING A DIAMOND AMONG THE COAL

U nlike buying a home, where almost every house is on the multiple listing service (MLS), the majority of small and midsized business buy-sell deals are done directly from seller to buyer. Statistics from numerous sources, including the International Business Brokers Association, say that 20–50 percent of profitable small to midsized businesses are never advertised or listed by a business broker. That means if you approach business buying like you would home buying, you are missing out on half or more of the market (this is not the case in larger, middle-market deals, where investment bankers represent the majority of deals).

In the 1980s, *Business Week* coined the term "hidden market" for small business sales, and it's as true today as it ever was. "Hidden market" is a common term in the job-search market, and as we'll see, there are many similarities between a business search and a job search and finding new customers for a business.

Your goal should be to pursue 100 percent of the market. If you don't, you are shortchanging yourself. Also, given the above and what follows, it means this:

The small to midsized business buy-sell market is extremely inefficient.

As mentioned, there is no MLS for businesses, where all companies for sale are available for easy viewing and comparing. Business brokers don't share listings or split commissions.

So where are they? Where are all these great acquisition candidates? They are everywhere, which is why it is so tough to find them. Even if there was a central listing service, it wouldn't help you much, given only 20–50 percent are advertised or sold by a broker; for middle-market firms, it's much higher, as most are represented by an investment bank. That means you must find the companies on the hidden market. That's why I say it's a sales effort. You and your employees are all acting like salespeople, except instead of prospecting for new customers, you are prospecting for business sellers.

The first and easiest place to start is with the business brokers and the M&A department of investment banking firms (the ones appropriate for your size deal). Call every intermediary you can find in every city in which you are willing to buy a company. Determine which companies work with the type and size of firm you are targeting. The key is to stay in touch. Call them once a month to let them know you're serious.

If you want to buy a company in your industry or a related industry, use your industry connections. Trade groups, professional groups, and professionals (accountants, consultants, attorneys, and others) can all be good sources. Start by contacting the national, regional, and local offices of any trade groups you belong to. If you aren't a member, join. If you aren't an active member, get active. Become known, especially to the executive director and key staff. When they see you do good work for the association, they will feel much better about helping you and referring companies to you.

You should also tell everybody you know that you are seeking to grow by acquisition. Don't be bashful; many deals are found because of the "people" factor. You never know who knows somebody who knows somebody who knows an owner wishing to retire or sell for other reasons.

One client found the business he bought by sending an e-mail to an alumni group. One of his fellow alumni forwarded it to others, and one of those recipients introduced him to an owner who not only wanted to sell but also sold to him.

Finally, realize that finding a business to buy is a contact sport. The more contacts you make, the better your chances of finding a company. Many years ago, an investment banker told me that the common impression of his profession was that it was always glamorous and exciting. He went on to say he spent most of his time at his desk "dialing for dollars"—in other words, working his contacts and others who might be able to help him. Get a list of target companies and contact them. Whether you write or call, make contacts.

Making contacts brings up an interesting point. Who makes all these contacts? You can. Or your management team can. But do you or your staff have the time? What about confidentiality? For example, if one of your competitors called you and asked if you were interested in merging or selling, what would you say? If you're like most owners, you would immediately say, "Not interested," because it could be a fishing expedition and that competitor could tell customers your business is for sale. What if you didn't know who was calling? Would you be any more relaxed about saying you'll discuss selling your business? This is a tough subject, isn't it?

That's where an intermediary comes into play. Somebody who does this work every day can better protect a seller's confidentiality. Since the business is based on keeping secrets, using an intermediary opens up doors to places you can't get into. I recommend you find an intermediary who does predominantly buy-side representation and works in the deal size range you are targeting. Industry knowledge most often takes a back seat to transaction knowledge. In addition, someone too well known in an industry may know too much or too many people. As Benjamin Franklin said, "Three people can keep a secret if two of them are dead." Getting an industry outsider on your team may be the smartest thing you do.

Disclaimer—what's described in the previous paragraph is what I do every day for clients, following my proven process.

The Org Chart of Search

As the following org chart of search shows, there are only three search strategies to find a business to buy. You must implement all three to maximize your chances of success.

You can be the best negotiator or analyst. However, if you don't have a company to analyze or a deal to negotiate, what use are those skills? In business, it all starts with making a sale, also known as getting a customer (or an order). In a business search, it all starts with finding companies, and the best way to ensure you will find one is to know what you want (and implement the plan to find it), as we covered in chapter 2 (nineteen reasons).

Seven Steps to a Successful Search

1. Define your criteria.
2. Gather your materials.
3. Assemble your A team.

4. Build relationships.
5. Know why the seller is selling.
6. Understand your search is your job.
7. Implement your search plan.

Step 1: Define Your Criteria

The following chart has seven key acquisition criteria (from the nineteen reasons). Give these, and other criteria, serious thought before embarking on your search.

Criteria	Your resources or feelings
Capital to invest	
Cash flow needed	
Seller role	
Location	
New product lines	
Acquire talent	
Customers	
Other	
Other	

Let me address only the first three, as the other criteria have already been covered.

Capital to Invest

Buying a business is trading your capital for immediate cash flow. The company you can afford to buy, the additional salary you may receive, and the growth of the company are all tied to the amount of money you have and how much of it you are willing to invest. You should rarely, if ever, invest "everything." You always want to have adequate reserves. As I write this, it is possible to buy a company (typically up to a $6–7 million deal) with as little as 10 percent down if the bank uses the SBA loan guarantee program (25 percent if it's a conventional bank loan).

Cash Flow

There are many definitions of cash flow, and as you'll find out in chapter 8, I don't like to use the term EBITDA (earnings before interest, taxes, depreciation, and amortization) because it can be extremely misleading (but it's become part of corporate and buy-sell vernacular, so I reference it, even though in small business sales, it's often misused). I like to use this definition, which is "free cash flow":

> Profit + owner salary + depreciation + nonbusiness expenses – capital expenditures – operating interest (line of credit) – fair market owner compensation

This cash flow should be at least two times the fair market salary for the job of running the company and preferably three or more times. Also, your starting point for acquisition debt payments should be 50 percent of profit (the cash flow less fair market owner salary). As mentioned, the larger the deal, the greater the flexibility you have with the 50 percent rule. This is a 2:1 debt coverage ratio ($2 of profit for every $1 of debt service minus principal and interest). Don't over-leverage. Even if the bank will allow you to use their minimum of a 1.25:1 debt coverage ratio, don't do it unless there are mitigating circumstances. In fact, good business-acquisition lenders won't want you under 1.5:1.

On smaller deals, especially if broker listed, you will often see the term "seller discretionary earnings (SDE)," "owner discretionary income," or some other variation. This includes salary, profit, perks, benefits, depreciation, and just about anything else that can be thrown into the formula. It's a way for brokers and others to avoid the discussion of what is the fair market owner salary for the business (the seller/broker thinks a $75,000-a-year manager can run the firm making $1 million, and the buyer believes it takes a $250,000-a-year person). If this number is being used, remember that, for valuation purposes, you can't use the same rules and techniques that you would for a profit figure. And I have never seen a bank or credible business appraiser use this number. They all use net income after fair market owner compensation.

Seller's Role and Activities

What does the seller do on a daily, weekly, and monthly basis? Individual buyers always tell me they want to be involved with strategy, vision, management, and leadership. But you have that covered, right?

So ask the seller, "What do you do on a daily basis?" and "What skills does someone need to take over your responsibilities?" This is our first insight into whether the business is a good fit for your team and you.

It's important that you define what you want to do and, early on in the process, find out what the seller does. A quick no is worth as much as a yes.

What if the seller wants to stay and work for you? Do you need her? Is there a dependency requiring her? As mentioned above, some sellers can't handle working for someone else. Others fit right in and are glad to "do the work" and not have to do any management.

Step 2: Gather Your Materials

Unlike an individual buyer, all you really need is a good one-sheet description of your target(s). It should tell a little about your company and you, give general parameters about what you are interested in, and provide contact information. Be as general as possible; you don't want anybody to deselect you (giving you a referral) because you were too specific.

Use this description as you do the following:

- Build a database of everybody you know, send them a notice that you are looking for a business to buy, and regularly send them updates of your search, including what you are analyzing, what your criteria are, and what you like and don't like.
- Consider a page on your website (homepage perhaps), mentioning your desire to buy another company. LinkedIn is also good for this.

- Post updates and requests on whatever social media vehicles you use (Facebook, Twitter, blog, LinkedIn, etc.).

Step 3: Assemble Your A-Team

Sellers don't want a buyer who won't use a team. So use your team to decrease your risk.

Buying a business is like climbing a mountain. There are ups, downs, dangerous crevices, and slippery slopes. If you're climbing by yourself, you may make it to the summit. If you are part of a team, your odds increase dramatically. If you have a team and an experienced guide who knows all the danger zones on the trek and how to avoid them, you have an excellent chance of reaching the summit safely.

As a business-buyer advocate, I often coordinate the team with the buyer. The usual suspects include the following:

- A transaction-savvy attorney who has done deals in the same size range as your deal
- A CPA who knows transaction tax and deal structure and can set up the financial systems and structure
- A banker who knows and likes acquisition loans and understands ongoing business banking needs.

The following also needs to be considered, as the deal requires (this list is not meant to be all inclusive):

- A CFO to assist with financial modeling, cash-flow projections, budgets, and management-reporting systems
- A human resources specialist to make sure the company's hiring and other employee policies are current and legal
- A commercial real-estate professional (there are now many who don't lease or list property and only work for the tenant, similar to what I do as a business-buyer advocate)
- An engineer for specific mechanical or structural issues

Real-Life Story: Have Advisors with the Right Experience

One of my clients told me that he just loved and very much respected his attorney. I questioned if the attorney was the right one, given that his firm was associated with upper-middle-market deals, not small-to-midsized-company deals. My client assured me all was OK.

His attorney drafted the purchase and sale agreement and sent it to the seller's attorney. The response was that they would not even read the agreement. They said they would take it upon themselves to write one more appropriate (kudos to them). Their agreement came back at one-third the size.

When I asked my client about this, he told me that his attorney had done such a great job for him in the past. When I probed, he confided that the other transaction was when he (my client) was the CEO of a firm that was involved with a complicated merger with a European company.

His attorney took his skills for large international deals and applied them to a small business deal. It just didn't work, and we were lucky the seller's attorney had the common sense not to work off and negotiate off the middle-market template.

Step 4: Build Relationships

Sometimes I think my clients get tired of me talking about how business buy-sell is a relationship game. What does this mean on a practical level? It means you have to be prepared for every meeting because you never know if it will be "the one." You must do the following:

- Have an opening statement.
- Be prepared with your questions for the seller.
- Have formulated answers for questions the seller may ask you.
- Be ready to end the meeting with a definitive next step (telephone call, sending of information, next in-person meeting, whatever).

Step 5: Know Why the Seller Is Selling?

This is an age-old question that raises skepticism in a buyer, and you will have to get good at (nicely) asking the tough questions to uncover the real reason. Unless there's a definitive event in the seller's life, buyers wonder why the seller would sell a profitable business. A seller stating that he wants to "pursue other interests" doesn't hold it with many buyers (although often it's true if the owner has been in the business a long time).

As one client (who had previously bought, grown, and sold a company) said to me, "The best time to sell a business is one year before you're burned out." Many investment managers don't hesitate to sell a stock when they feel it's the right time.

While it creates urgency, there usually isn't a catastrophic event that forces a sale. Divorce, death, and disability aren't common reasons. Business owners are like everybody else. In corporate America, people change jobs every three to five years. Owners last longer, but they do have other ideas and interests. The smart owner will sell before getting completely burned out, when the business is doing well and when she can demonstrate future growth is possible.

As we'll see later, buyers are attracted to companies when they see areas where they can add (immediate) value. All of this said, a healthy degree of skepticism is not only expected; it's encouraged. One can never be too careful (and the same should go for a seller's skepticism of the buyer and his abilities).

The reasons for selling that you should look for include the following. Most deals I see are burnout or retirement, with something like a health issue compounding the situation.

- Death
- Disability

- Divorce
- Partner/shareholder or family dispute
- Burnout
- Retirement
- Health (owner or spouse)
- Life
- Entrepreneur owner (who wants to start another business rather than manage the current one)

Step 6: Understand Your Search Is Your Job

A successful search starts with having a plan and implementing the plan (the strategies in the org chart of business search). This is no different than finding a job, prospecting for a new customer, or even dating. If you have a plan and implement it, you will be more successful than if you don't. However, even the smartest business buyers often neglect this step. For some reason, all of the business acumen disappears when it comes to doing a search for a business.

This could be because buying a business is not like buying a house, but buying a house is what most of us have done more than once. The following provides details on the major differences.

This following quote is from Richard Parker (www.diomo.com), one of America's foremost experts on business buy-sell:

It's amazing how, regardless of the level of sophistication, experience, and business acumen of a prospective business buyer, the acquisition process always seems "easy" to those who have never experienced it.

Richard wrote this to me during an e-mail exchange we had about business buyers (in general). Too many of the buyers Richard describes think buying a business is like buying a house. My point here is that you need to make sure your team and you have the bandwidth to do a search (plus due diligence, working with the bank, and the legal aspects) as you run your current business. In addition, your team must have the time to integrate the target firm into your operations.

Step 7: Implement Your Search Plan
As mentioned previously, there are only three strategies you can use to find a business for sale, and all are important. Buyers who consistently and regularly implement all three strategies have a greater chance of finding a target company and doing so quicker.

Public Market
These days, the Internet has taken over as the advertising vehicle of choice. Take a look at the businesses advertised here, and you'll get frustrated. You'll also realize most of the businesses advertised, especially the good businesses, are represented by business brokers.

Realize brokers often don't initially put their best listings on these websites; they work their database first. Why? So they don't get inundated with calls from unqualified buyers.

The biggest mistake buyers make is not staying in touch with brokers. Their second mistake is not building a relationship with the brokers. They call a few times, and if there are no listings that match, they give up (on that broker). It's important that you keep in touch with all the brokers who handle deals in the size range you are targeting and they get to know you. They're people too and want to do deals with people they like.

I have a great relationship with my local (Seattle) business brokers. I can chalk up many deals to these relationships, as brokers like working with my clients because they know my clients are qualified and realistic (I don't work with bottom-feeders trying to steal a company). Here's an example:

Real-Life Story: Stay in Touch; There Are Many Ways Businesses Are Marketed

A business broker told me that after securing a listing, the client asked if he'd be marketing it "everywhere." His reply was that no, he wouldn't do that. Instead, he would make five telephone calls. If he didn't find a good buyer, he would make five more calls and keep making calls until he was successful. He did this because he didn't want the business's name out in public to all the unqualified buyers who answer ads. I was one of his first five calls, and one of my clients was a good fit and bought the business.

Network, Network, Network

Networking is something the majority of business buyers do

- right after they start attacking the public market of companies for sale,
- an incomplete job of and poorly, or
- so inadequately, they wonder why they aren't getting a lot of referrals.

Many business buyers have not been involved in business development during their careers. They have been managers and leaders and therefore don't completely understand the process of networking (and marketing in general).

In step 2, I listed the materials you should have to conduct a viable search. Materials are great, and social media is a fairly new tool, but neither are substitutes for face-to-face meetings. You have to meet with people to make your best impression.

Real-Life Story: Finding a Business Is a Contact Sport

Many years ago, at a professional group meeting, a crusty old salesman pulled me, a young marketing neophyte, aside and drew the following picture on a piece of paper.

He asked me if I knew what the drawing was. I didn't know, and he told me that no matter what the circumstances, the best way to make a sale was to get belly to belly (the drawing represents two people standing belly to belly).

Fast-forward many years, and meeting people one on one is still the best way to communicate and get the results you want, especially for business buyers.

Search, Regroup, Search, Repeat

So who do you connect with? The answer, as stated above, is everybody you know.

Start by putting together a list of family, friends, business associates, alumni, and others, such as your dentist, doctor, CPA, and other service providers. Your second step is to rank them using a simple A, B, C system. All can receive e-mails at the same time, but prioritize in-person meetings. Realize you can't meet with too many people. This is a numbers game, and the more people you contact, the better your chances of success.

From now on, every breakfast, coffee, and lunch meeting not specific to company operations should be related to your search. Seek out trade groups, chambers of commerce, networking events, and professional associations, as they are all viable situations. Don't be afraid to get to the point. This is not a time to be wishy-washy. Tell people your objective point-blank, which is to buy a mature, profitable business.

Then stay in touch. A weak link in networking (all networking, not just as part of a business search) is the lack of staying in touch. I suggest an e-mail every month that gives a summary of your activities, mentions companies you have looked at, and reminds people that your objective is to buy a business, so ask them to please refer to you any situations where the owner may be even thinking of selling. Here is what one client sent as part of his update (and notice it's in the postscript because that is the second-most read part of any letter or message, after the headline or opening sentence).

> P.S. As a reminder, I'm searching for a small company with a defensible niche position in the greater San Francisco area. My ideal acquisition target is a manufacturing or distribution company in a mature industry with $5M to $12M in annual revenues and an owner who wants to exit. Here is a link to my acquisition website.

As a business-buyer advocate, I also network on behalf of all my clients, and every time I track results, the deals that are found via networking are at about a fifty-fifty split between my clients' and mine. Mine come from my established network, and theirs come from getting out and meeting people (one recent deal was a referral from someone in my network whose name I gave to my client so he could make the contact). About half of businesses referred to clients are from people they didn't know when they started searching.

People like to help other people, especially people they know and like. That's why you shouldn't be hesitant to directly ask for their help or to stay in touch. There is also a give-to-get karma on this planet, so anytime you can help someone else, do so. In fact, when you meet with people and are asking for their assistance to help you find a company to buy, ask if there is anything you can do for them or someone you can introduce them to. I built a network of over one hundred referral sources from a base of three within one year by asking for names of other professionals, and as I started meeting those people, I then offered to introduce them to others.

Be Proactive
The third way to find a business to buy is to target industries and reach out to companies to see if they are interested in selling. There are many owners who are thinking of selling, and if your timing is right, you just may find a prospective seller.

Many owners (sellers) I talk with just don't know what to do and are scared to death regarding confidentiality or the lack of it. One of your biggest obstacles when prospecting directly to companies is confidentiality. If owners tell you they are interested in discussing selling their company, for all they know, you are with a competitor who will use that information in the marketplace. As a shameless plug for using a business-buyer advocate (me), when I contact an owner, I can impress upon him or her my ability to hold secrets. If word gets out that an intermediary violated confidentiality, that person is out of business.

So owners who don't know how to sell keep operating the business, even if the drive and passion are slipping away. You probably want to ask, "Why wouldn't they call some business brokers and put the business on the market?" Here are three reasons many owners have shared with me.

1. Confidentiality is again on the top of the list. Owners fear that, even with confidentiality agreements, word will get out because a broker's job is to market the business. This may be unfounded (as good brokers are very careful), but it is a fear.
2. They don't know whom to call. There's a wide range of deal sizes, and the International Business Brokers Association says that the average price of broker-sold businesses is about $300,000 (this is also quoted in statistics provided by bizbuysell.com). When owners look on the Internet, they see the majority of businesses for sale are small, and that bothers them. If they expect to get seven or eight figures for their business, they fear working with someone who is out of their league with their size company. It's the same reason they use a CPA for taxes and not the tax preparer in the kiosk at the mall.
3. The few people who use manipulative techniques to get a listing have tainted the brokerage industry. Here's how it goes, and every owner has experienced this or heard about it from a friend. A broker cold-calls an owner and tells her they have a buyer for her business. The owner goes to the broker's office and finds out she has to sign a listing agreement to meet the buyer, and when she does, she is told the buyer was looking for something

in the industry (say manufacturing in general), not her particular business. Usually, the buyer is not interested or qualified. It's called fishing for a listing, and I regularly get asked if I am fishing for a listing even after I convey I don't list businesses. Good brokers don't do this, but they all get lumped together.

Real-World Example

Twice within a week or so, these two things happened. A client called and told me a broker indicated he had an upcoming listing. My client figured out the company very quickly. You see, there are only so many manufacturers of "restaurant furniture" in any city.

Then another client called and told me about a similar experience. Only this time, the broker indicated he would be listing a company that is owned by a client of mine. Given the company's niche, it was easy to figure out. Not only did that owner not want to sell, he wanted to buy another business.

Using the criteria previously discussed, we come up with a list of target companies and reach out to them. You will do this by letter, e-mail, and telephone. Based on your criteria, your skills, and your interest, pick industries that seem to be a match.

After sending letters, you may want to send them again, to the same people, if you don't hear from enough owners with good, profitable businesses. However, you will have to pick up the telephone and call everybody you sent the letter to in order to maximize your results.

Here is a script for telephoning owners. Adapt this if you have to leave a voice-mail message. Under no circumstances should you tell anybody else in the firm why you are calling. Your saying nothing more than that you are looking to buy a business will start rumors flying that the company is for sale.

Ms. or Mr. Owner, this is (your name), and I'm looking for a business to buy in your industry. I recently sent you a letter but didn't hear from you, so I decided to call to see if you are interested in discussing selling your business or, if not, if you know of someone who may be interested in selling.

Remember, it's a numbers game and a timing game. Owners not interested in selling now may be interested in four months. If we make a good impression, they will remember us and call when the time is right.

Your search is the most critical component of business buying. There is nothing else you can do if you haven't found any businesses interested in discussing selling. You dramatically increase your chances of success if you are active with all three of the search strategies. Stay in touch with the appropriate brokers, network efficiently and effectively, and proactively contact owners.

Finally, realize if you are calling competitors, they will be very hesitant to speak with you. Even if they do, they will be scared to share detailed information about their sales, margins, profit, people, etc. Just like prospecting for customers, you keep doing the right things the right way, over and over and over. Do what you're supposed to do, and good things will happen.

Why They Made an Acquisition

Jim Creagan is the second-generation owner of Randob Labs in Cornwall, New York, www.randob.com. As I write this, Jim and I are working together to find a company to acquire. Randob has three over-the-counter (OTC) pharmaceutical products they manufacture and distribute. We are looking for companies with other OTC products or other distribution channels (for Randob's products).

Here are three tips from Jim:

- Don't buy just to buy. Know what you want and target those firms. Besides products and channels, Jim will consider companies with operational or marketing issues he can improve.

- Take stock of what you do and do well. Know what you offer the marketplace.
- Use the process to also conduct market research. He learned there are hundreds of companies in his industry doing well. Talking to the owners and seeing information confirmed to him what he's doing right.

Jim also told me it didn't surprise him how many lifestyle businesses are out there (a business that's really a job paying a good salary and not much more) because it's a leap from being a founder (with a great idea) to running a real business. What did surprise him was the lack of good accounting systems (this was not a surprise to me).

Jim's reasons for an acquisition are some of the most common. He wants a larger company, more products, more reach, and structure.

CHAPTER 6

SHOW ME THE MONEY—AND WHEN DO I GET IT?

Money—a subject of many songs (The Beatles, Pink Floyd, Cabaret Soundtrack, Monty Python, and many more artists), stories, and conflicts. When it comes to buying a small to mid-sized company (not middle market), there are some givens. They include the following:

- You will put in some of your funds as (part of) the down payment.
- Banks will want to finance your deal (assuming it makes economic sense).
- The bank will want collateral (SBA loans and some conventional loans are "cash-flow" lenders, meaning they don't require 100 percent collateral coverage).
- There's a good chance you will sign a personal guarantee.
- There should be some seller financing.
- Cash flow is king. The more cash flow, the greater the chances of getting financing. (Refer to the section on cash flow and debt-coverage ratios.)

Let's address these points. As it says, you will put in some of your own funds. It is rare a business buyer can buy another company without any of their cash being used, unless it's a distressed company. In that case, it may require cash to pay off liabilities. If your target company is profitable, figure you'll be putting in at least 10 percent of the purchase price and perhaps 25 percent (any more is up to you).

Different Rules for Different Situations

Distressed companies have different rules. Stu bought a firm in trouble because they expanded too fast via starting remote locations. He was the knight in shiny armor to the seller, although the seller received no money at closing (there was an earn out). The down payment went to the state's department of revenue for back taxes, the primary vendor, and the phone company.

Conventional versus SBA Loans

I previously mentioned how some banks love acquisition loans, some don't do them, and some are lukewarm about them. This is why it's important to work with a bank that is bullish on acquisition loans. I have clients who absolutely love their bank for ongoing banking needs. But those banks are not the ones they used when it came to an acquisition.

There is no pattern or formula here; it's all based on the bank officer's experience and familiarity with these loans. Ask your bank and any banks you're referred to how many acquisition loans they do, what requirements they have, etc. If a banker uses the term "blue sky" to describe goodwill, be careful and probe deeply. If they use the term "air ball" to describe goodwill, there's a 99 percent chance they won't do an acquisition loan. It means they are collateral-based, not cash-flow lenders (and not comfortable with the cash-flow lending concept). One of the questions you definitely want to ask is about the bank's collateral requirements. See the appendices for an essay on SBA lending by my friend Lisa Forrest, an SBA lender with Live Oak Bank.

Now let's quickly look at ten key features and compare conventional loans and SBA loans. For more on current SBA loan policies and information requirements, see the appendices.

1. **Collateral**

   Conventional loan refers to a standard bank loan. Many banks will want full collateral coverage (think real estate or equipment), personal assets, and probably a personal guarantee. SBA loans have much different collateral requirements. The bank, using the SBA program, will take first position on whatever assets they can. They will then take some personal assets, usually home equity. As an aside, this discriminates against borrowers with a large amount of home equity and is why I, and some bankers, recommend getting a home equity line of credit before starting the process so the bank/SBA is behind your current obligations. Most banks won't take investments, stocks, bonds, mutual funds, and similar. They probably will take a position on a vacation home or rental property, and they will want a personal guarantee (which is why private equity firms, investor-funded deals, and similar don't use SBA loans). But—and this is important—they don't need 100 percent collateral coverage. They are a cash-flow lender when using the SBA program, and this means the cash flow (i.e., debt coverage) is considered an asset.

2. **Interest Rate**

   The interest rate on SBA loans will usually be higher. On recent deals, one with a conventional loan and two with an SBA loan, the interest rate on the conventional loan was 1.25–1.5 percent lower than the SBA rate. On another deal, two banks offered a phenomenal SBA rate to the owner of a business buying another one in the same industry. The reason for this low rate was the strength of his existing company and the positive cash flow of the target firm.

3. **Term of Loan**

   A conventional loan's most common term is five years, sometimes with a longer amortization period (seven years more often than not), with a balloon payment at the end of five years. This is where the SBA program takes over, as they offer a ten-year amortization, which keeps the payments much lower (even with the higher interest rate).

4. **Cash Outlay**

   With a conventional loan, expect your cash outlay to be 25 percent of the price. SBA loans are different. As of this writing, late 2017, the word is the 2018 SBA policy will be 10 percent down from the buyer. Quite a difference (and there are some related policies, and as they're not in force yet, I won't comment here).

5. **Diligence**

   As previously mentioned, the banks are asking a lot of questions these days. It's my experience banks using the SBA program will collect and analyze more information than conventional lenders. It's because they will have to prove to the SBA they dotted their I's and crossed their T's if the loan has problems.

6. **Fees**

   The fees on SBA loans are significantly more—at this time, about 3 percent versus 1–1.25 percent. These fees get rolled into the loan. There are also fees for a business valuation, home appraisal, and packaging. The SBA percentage fee is really an insurance premium to cover the SBA's guarantee to the bank. (As of this writing, the SBA loan program is in the black.)

7. **Prepayment Penalties**

   SBA acquisition loans don't have a prepayment penalty (SBA real-estate loans often do). Conventional loans may or may not have a penalty; it varies from bank to bank.

8. **Seller Financing**

   The banks like the seller to have "skin in the game," and so should you. A client's recent deal with a conventional loan, with 25 percent down, still had a 10 percent seller note.

9. **Earn-out**

   Conventional loans have no restrictions on earn outs. SBA loans do. Technically, you can't have an earn out with an SBA loan, at least not a traditional earn out where there's a fixed price and the price goes up if certain metrics are met. What you can have (as of this writing) is a "negative earn out," also known as a "negative seller note," meaning you can have a price that goes down if certain metrics aren't met. However, the higher price must meet the bank's debt-coverage ratio requirements from day one (as if the full price will be paid from the start).

10. **Miscellaneous**

SBA loans are for US citizens and green-card holders. A background check is also required, and a felony may disqualify the applicant.

You Want How Much Information?

The bank will ask for a lot of information. My best clients and those with the most success getting offers from banks have taken the time to put together a book for each bank. They used to use a three-ring binder with tab dividers, but now it's all done electronically. They provide the bank with the following:

- Business financials (three years)
- Business tax returns (three years)
- Personal net worth statement (often on the bank's form)
- Personal-tax returns (one to three years)
- Short business plan
- Buyer's bio with accomplishments, not just jobs
- Letter from the seller on why the buyer is a good fit
- Reference letters from friends
- Other information on the business, including asset descriptions, AR and AP aging, customer list and concentration, org chart, and management duties and bios
- Pro forma P&L and balance sheet (the balance sheet is very important to banks) with realistic projections including if the first year is the same as the seller's last year and one projection with mild growth
- Monthly P&Ls for the last year and monthly cash-flow projections

Finally, I would be remiss to not mention the five Cs of banking. Banks have, to varying degrees, lived by them for decades.

Whether you are dependent on a bank or not, pay attention to this because the chances are your future buyer will need a bank to fund operations and growth, and the more your business is attractive to a bank, the more confident a buyer will be (meaning a better price, better terms, easier process, and perhaps a quicker payoff to you).

1. **Capacity**
   How will you repay the money? There had better be cash flow to support your debt payments, or why would anybody lend you the money? You'll be dependent on the next factor.

2. **Collateral**
   What does the lender get if you can't make the payments? Believe me, the bank does not want your truck, house, car, equipment, or anything else. They want to be repaid, and this is why they severely discount the value of the assets used as collateral.

3. **Capital**
   This is your skin in the game, also known as your risk. Your skin in the game (as an owner, buyer, or seller) is more important than it was in recent years.

4. **Conditions**
   What is the loan for? Banks usually want to tie long-term needs (a piece of equipment or a business acquisition) to a term loan. Short-term needs (working capital) will be tied to a line-of-credit loan like an accounts receivable line of credit that will be paid back when your customer pays you.

5. **Character**
   As when you sell your product or sell your business, it's a relationship game with your banker. You must come across as competent, trustworthy, experienced, and as having a solid reputation.

Creative Finance

Creative finance is not hocus-pocus or wishful thinking. It is using the cash flow or the assets of the business to help pay for the business or to pay yourself back (after closing). How common is it? Not nearly as common as it was before the current SBA rules (on deals under about $7 million). Here are a few examples (this is not a book on finance; for that, you should check out my friend Ted Leverette's book *How to Get All the Money You Want without Stealing It,* http://partneroncall.com/creative-financing/).

- Robb's company had extreme, and predictable, seasonality—about six months of being very busy and six months of slow sales. The seller understood this and agreed to finance a large portion of the deal with two payment amounts. For the busy season, the payments were 50 percent more (than a fixed amortization payment), and in the slow season they were 50 percent less.
- The deal had some moving parts. There was the issue of seasonality with four months a year having negative cash flow and the deal closing just before this slow season; then there was the fact the industry was economy centric, and the buyer was buying during an up-cycle, and finally, the inventory system wasn't very good, especially considering there were over eight thousand SKUs, and about twenty-five hundred of them had only one item in stock. This deal solved the problem with the following:
  (a) The inclusion of cash in the transferred assets, enough cash to cover the negative cash flow.
  (b) An earn-out structure for about 20 percent of the price, contingent on hitting gross profit numbers the first three years.
  (c) Inventory adjustments to cover items not usable and salable, in this case anything having not sold in the past year.
- When there's the issue of huge customer concentration, often some form of erosion or claw-back clause is used. The buying entity was, naturally, concerned because one customer was well over 50 percent of the annual sales. Now, this customer had been buying for fifteen years and growing annually, paid annually in advance, and had given positive indications they would continue buying more and more. So, the deal had a fixed payment equal

to 75 percent of the price, and the other 25 percent would be paid when the top customer made their next annual payment, which they made.

- I've had many buyers work with their bank to use a line of credit as part of the acquisition financing package. One buyer was a former banker, and he put together his own structure, which his bank agreed with. It involved a few different loans, one of which was a line of credit. Another deal had the banker use the firm's existing line of credit to pay for the acquisition (of a complementary product line). The banker simply expanded the line to its maximum amount, and the company drew on that line. The paperwork was less, the fees were low, and it provided flexible payments. This is a much more viable structure when it's one business buying another versus an individual buyer.

- Craig gambled; that's the easiest way to say it. His target was a bookkeeping mess, to put it mildly. After spending some time sifting through the mess, he made the sellers the offer of "I take everything as is." He took the cash, work in progress, accounts receivable, accounts payable, everything. Did he win? Yep, especially when he found over $100,000 of unbilled work (job summaries found in the pile of paperwork, along with uncashed checks).

- If the seller has a topline number in mind, sometimes it doesn't pay to negotiate it if it's possible to pay with tax-deductible methods. My favorite story is when Rick, the owner of three businesses, bought a fourth. His seller had a number, and we met the number by making a chunk of the deal consulting and employment agreements. All were immediately tax deductible. The seller didn't care if this was ordinary income and some self-employment taxes because he got "bragging rights."

Banks Want to Lend More, Not Less

The buyer got bank approval and was surprised by the total amount of the loan on his $4 million deal. It was as follows:

- Acquisition loan: $3,000,000
- Working capital: $350,000
- Extra cash: $125,000
- Total: $3,475,000

The banker's comment about the extra cash was "You'll need money to pay your closing costs, and it never hurts to have extra cash." Remember, bankers get paid based on the amount they lend.

Deal Structure

Let's cover eight topics, realizing there are a multitude of other things that are important to any deal but not major issues. I will cover the basics, as every deal is different, and your advisors will counsel you on the intricacies of your deal structure.

Stock Sale versus Asset Sale

First comment, these are tax-structure terms more than anything else. Whether it's structured as an asset sale or stock sale, you get the same things. What I mean by this is you get all assets, tangible and intangible. An asset sale can include liabilities, and a stock sale can exclude certain assets or peg them to an amount (e.g., $500,000 of cash will stay in the company). It does not mean, as many people think, you only get the assets you can touch, like furniture, fixtures, equipment, and vehicles (FFE&V) and inventory.

A stock sale is when you buy the stock of a corporation or the shares of an LLC. You get any and everything, including assets, liabilities, warranties, past tax obligations (known or unknown at the time of sale), everything. As mentioned, certain things may be pegged to an amount, so if there's more cash or working capital at closing, the seller takes it, and if there's less, the seller makes it whole (to be covered in more details later).

A stock sale, on the surface, is simpler. The seller signs his shares, and they're yours, just like stock in a publicly traded company. In reality, there are almost as many moving parts as with an asset sale. Your legal due diligence increases exponentially, due diligence in general increases, as you are buying "everything," and the representations and warranties section of the contract will be much more detailed. On the flip side, the administrivia of closing is greatly reduced. You don't have to change bank accounts, utility bills, vendor accounts, or anything else.

Why do a stock sale? The most common reason is the target company is a C corporation. If it is, there's the issue of double taxation. The money gets taxed at the corporate level and then again at the personal level when withdrawn. Sellers don't want to pay about 50 percent total tax instead of 20 percent capital gains tax (plus state taxes), which is what the seller pays with a stock sale if it is an S corporation, having flow through (to personal) money and therefore capital gains tax rates. Another reason is if the selling company has a large number of contracts or sensitive contracts.

Examples

The selling firm leased apartments long term and did short-term corporate rentals to companies bringing new employees to town, customers in for training, etc. They had three hundred leases. In an asset sale, each would have had to have been redone. With a stock sale, they transferred over.

In another case, the selling firm was a C corporation, and to make matters worse, they owned the real estate, which was in the corporation, not in a separate entity. Unraveling this was impossible; it had to be a stock sale.

An asset sale is when you buy a collection of assets. You can buy all the assets or just some of them, and you can also get liabilities. You will need to change vendor agreements, bank accounts, customer agreements, equipment leases, etc. Yes, it's a lot of paperwork, but it's worth it, and not just from the reduced liability perspective (your lawyer can handle covering you with protections).

What you get with an asset sale is the ability to redepreciate the assets and to amortize the goodwill over fifteen years. Not a bad paper write-off to reduce taxes. You can also allocate part of the price to transition training and deduct it as paid (realize the seller pays ordinary income-tax rates on this).

My opinion, and that of the legal and tax professionals I know, is an asset sale is almost always preferable for the buyer.

Why a C Corporation

There are only a couple of good reasons a small business is a C corporation. First, if the owner used qualified money to start or buy the firm, it has to be a C corporation. There's a clause in the IRS regulations that allows people to use qualified money to buy (or start) a business without paying tax or penalty. One of the regulations mandates the entity be a C corporation.

Another reason is legacy earnings. A long-established company may have certain earnings virtually requiring it to remain a C corporation (there used to be many good reasons to be a C not an S corporation, and almost all of those reasons have gone away). If converting to an S corporation would trigger a massive event, the company won't change. (Disclaimer: I'm not a CPA or tax expert; consult your CPA on this.)

The bad reasons for remaining a C corporation are simple: a bad CPA or inertia. Rarely is it the CPA, and if it is, it's usually because he doesn't pay attention to the big picture; he is just doing taxes. Most likely, it's an owner ignoring advice from her CPA. That's inertia, resistance to change even when change is highly beneficial.

Stock Sale Avoidance

There's a way around the stock sale issue if it's a C corporation and the deal is small enough.

If the deal is under $3 million or so, you can use the personal goodwill, versus company goodwill, concept commonly referred to as the Martin Ice Cream case structure. In simple terms (check with your CPA or your attorney), there are two transactions. First, you purchase, from the company, stock or assets up to basis. Then you purchase goodwill directly from the seller, structured as an asset sale. You get the write-offs, and he gets the capital gains tax rate. Get too much over $3 million, and you'll have a hard time proving the owner is really that critical to the company to justify personal goodwill.

There's one other technique: a section 338h10 transaction structure. However, it only applies to S corporations, so if you need to do a stock sale to keep contracts in place, you can still get the asset sale benefits.

Terms

This used to be much more important than it is now. There was always leverage between price and terms. Now, your seller, you, and your respective advisors all know the banks are standing in line to make acquisition loans. If you're above the SBA threshold, there is a bit more opportunity to negotiate how and when the seller gets paid. If it's all seller financing, it's one thing (good for you, if you can get this). But if it's just a matter of a small or large bank loan, I don't see much difference, other than bank fees. On the hook to the bank for $3 million or $4 million, not much difference.

Terms also includes a description of what you're buying or, more important, what, if anything, is excluded. In general terms, you get everything except the seller's personal items. This means furniture, fixtures, equipment, and vehicles (FFE&V), plus inventory and working capital (more on this later). It can include the transfer of contracts and leases, transition support, employment or a consulting agreement with the seller, and the noncompete agreement (more on this later).

Conditions to Closing

These can be the necessary components of the deal, plus anything the seller or you want included. Some of the necessary components are the following:

- Completion of due diligence, including customer, employee, and vendor discussions.
- Financing approval.
- Employment agreements, especially if there are already agreements.
- No material adverse changes to the business or its relationships.
- No shop clause for the seller (you have exclusive rights for a set amount of time).
- Environmental clearance.

Noncompete

Your seller is going to sign a noncompete and nonsolicitation agreement (they can't approach your employees or customers). Even if she's retiring and in poor health, she'll sign one. Your attorney will advise you on what's acceptable in your state. My experience is it's tough to get one for more than five years, but there are exceptions. This may also include a geographic area, which could be as small as a five-mile radius to worldwide. Bottom line, if you are worried about the seller becoming your competition, you might want to rethink doing a deal with this person.

Earn Out

A litigator's dream come true is another way to describe an earn out. That said, I like earn outs for the right situation. In simple terms, an earn out is when part of the price is based on future performance. It could be a sharing of profits (easy to manipulate by the buyer), of sales (can be tough on the buyer if the business makes a large-volume, low-margin sale), or of gross profit (often the preferred metric).

The right situation is not the buyer wanting to pay a fair price but not guaranteeing 100 percent of it or the seller wanting an earn out on top of the fair price just to get more. Good uses for an earn out include when the company has a new product just coming to market, the company or the industry has cycles (don't buy on top with no protection), or a (supposed) singular event has depressed the company's current valuation.

Working Capital

If you're buying a very small business or a retail business, you're probably not going to get any working capital other than inventory. If you're buying a larger firm and especially a B2B company, you should expect to get usual and customary working capital. This is often called a "cash-free, debt-free" deal structure. The seller keeps the cash and pays off the long-term debt, including the current portion of said debt. After that, a usual starting point is to figure out the average working capital, often defined as the training twelve months average of accounts receivable plus inventory plus WIP less accounts payable and accrued liabilities. If the company has work in process, especially with customer deposits, it's a much different and more complicated calculation.

This gives the buyer the working capital to adequately run the business from day one and offers protections to both parties. The buyer is protected against the seller accelerating AR or delaying paying his AP to generate retained cash. The seller is not penalized for having a big sales month or two prior to closing, as he will keep AR over the average.

Representations and Warranties

I'm not going to discuss any of the legalities regarding representations (reps) and warranties. I'll just give you the business and deal perspective. Buyer and seller will both sign an agreement filled with reps and warranties. You will represent and warranty everything you told the seller about yourself and your business is true and correct, including your company's financial statements.

The seller will rep and warranty a lot more (i.e., everything about the business from the financial statements to legal issues, customer lists, environmental issues, and anything else). In simple terms, the seller is responsible for anything that happened prior to closing, and you are responsible for what happens after closing.

This all sounds reasonable and normal, doesn't it? Here's where it can get sticky and where the lawyers have to play well together. Sometimes the seller or her attorney will want to put in a phrase like "to the best of seller's knowledge" in front of the words "seller (or shareholder, stockholder, etc.) represents and warranties the following." You can see the room for ambiguity (and deception), and your attorney won't like this.

You don't want to be in a situation where the seller can say, "I had no knowledge of this," and be off the hook. In a small to midsized business, the owner should, and does, have knowledge of everything. I have seen situations where the seller wouldn't sign without the knowledge clause, and it only confirmed the buyer's feelings regarding trustworthiness. I have heard about a couple of deals where the seller wouldn't sign any reps and warranties, and it then came out he was lying about what he'd presented to the buyer.

This is the area where the lawyers spend the largest amount of time, other than writing the agreement. Is it important? Yes, very important, especially when it comes to indemnification regarding the reps and warranties. Does it come into play often? No. In my twenty-plus years as an intermediary, I've seen only a few instances of claims against the reps and warranties, and one was a self-inflicted wound by the buyer (he ignored my advice, his attorney's advice, and his own common sense and didn't do the recommended due diligence on the issue that came back to bite him, which he would have uncovered if he had done things properly). An attorney I know told me he's had three in thirty-three years.

But you still have to protect yourself as much as possible. And as with the noncompete, if the seller won't sign a tight agreement on this, you have to wonder what's going on.

Why They Made an Acquisition

Mayumi Nakamura is the CEO of Pacific Software Publishing Inc. (www.pspinc.com), a Bellevue, Washington, website-hosting and related services company that has made numerous acquisitions. As you know, website hosting is a low-priced service that must be done right, or there are huge ramifications.

PSP can't afford six-figure salespeople to sell $100–200-a-year services. So their primary objective is to get more customers they can plug into their system and work with on additional services.

Mayumi likes unwinding the company, analyzing it, and then putting the pieces back together. With her firm, the technology is one of the key components. When it comes together the right way, it's a deal that makes sense, and that means the more you work on the details, the easier it is to assimilate the other firm.

Her advice to others is to make sure the deal makes sense, that it doesn't just *sound* good. Also, the other firm (and its owner) must be in sync with your values, or you'll have more problems than benefits. This means assess all the risks so you know how to deal with them before closing.

CHAPTER 7

THE EMOTIONAL ROLLER COASTER

Often ignored yet probably the most important aspect of any buy-sell deal is the emotional stress both parties are under. In chapter 3, I discussed the importance of a solid relationship between buyer and seller, and it bears repeating here. This is a relationship game, and a solid relationship between buyer and seller leads to a smaller emotional roller coaster. When there's trust, there's confidence the right decision is being made.

Business buyers, whether it's a first-time buyer or a seasoned veteran, are always "on the fence." Should I do this or not? Should I ask more questions, or do I have enough information? The tighter the relationship, the less of a balancing act, for both buyer and seller.

I've been told, by many clients, that one of the greatest values I've provided them is the ability to talk through issues, to listen, and to provide "been there, done that" insights. Sometimes convincing the buyer to do nothing (about a touchy situation) is the best path because often these issues solve themselves. More often, rather than offering a solution, the best course of action is to ask the seller how he would handle it if he were in your position.

Often, I'm pulling the buyer back, making him realize he has enough information to make a decision. But sometimes it doesn't work, as the following story demonstrates.

Real-Life Example

The buyer was an extremely inquisitive person, and he loved to negotiate. In fact, he once asked me if I thought the seller would "want to haggle a lot." When I responded no, he was disappointed. But this was his style, and it manifested itself with the asking of (too many) questions. The seller even nicknamed him Columbo (after the old TV show) because, like Columbo, he always had "one more question." It got to the point where his attorney and I cautioned him about this, and the seller's attorney called me to discuss this trait of his, as it finally went from charming to irritating. The seller wanted a decision, not another question.

Occasionally, I have to push my clients to ask more questions. My most extreme example was a buyer named Michael. I had to have a serious talk with him about his lack of due diligence. His response was he trusted everything the seller said so there was no real need to prove it with further investigation. We compromised; he did some diligence, moved on to closing, and all went well postsale, no surprises.

Buyer Emotions

Business buyers' emotional angst is concentrated on two main questions.

1. Am I getting what I think I'm getting?
2. Am I inheriting things I don't want?

Let's break down the first question into the top five components.

- Is the cash flow what I hope and think it is?
- Will the customers stay?
- Will the employees leave or demand a lot more money?

- Will the vendors stay with me and extend the same credit terms?
- Is this truly a sustainable business model I can grow? And if it's growth by acquisition, can we integrate the culture and operations?

Cash Flow

In the next chapter, I'll cover different cash-flow terminologies, what they mean, where the traps are, and what's truly usable cash flow. For a buyer, the real issue comes down to one question: Will the cash flow I get be the same or better than what the seller claims it is? Sellers and their representatives are notorious for adding everything, including the proverbial kitchen sink, to their cash-flow calculations.

These "add-backs" can include depreciation (ignoring ongoing capital expenditures); interest; owner benefits like cell phones, medical insurance, pension contributions, and more; marketing campaigns that "didn't work"; the salary of an employee the seller says can be let go; and, of course, the owner's salary.

With the last item, it's amazing how little the sellers often do in the business when it is time to sell versus the bragging they do to their friends about how the business can't survive without them.

Customer Retention

The inability to retain customers is a common yet usually irrational fear. Customers want to be taken care of. They want the service they're accustomed to, or better, and, most important, they don't like change. One of the last things a company wants to do is have to find a new supplier, especially when things are running smoothly.

Employee Retention

This is the big fear, and it's a fear buyers, sellers, and employees share. As the three-legged stool diagram in chapter 3 shows, all parties are scared one of the others will kick out their leg of the stool; it will collapse, and the employees will lose their jobs.

Yet everybody involved wants job security and stability. The seller wants the buyer to take care of her people, and as mentioned in chapter 4, buyers are buying the people more than anything else. At the same time, the employees want to keep their jobs; they don't like change, even more than customers don't. Of course, a change in ownership is often used to ask for a raise.

The Flip Side

The absentee owner firm had two high-priced managers, to the tune of a total comp package of about $200,000 each. One was the CFO, and I use the term lightly, and the other was the CEO. During diligence, everybody—meaning the bank, buyer, and I—figured the CFO could be replaced with someone earning about $100,000. Within a few months, this is what happened.

The CEO position was a little trickier, as there wasn't too much knowledge about what she did. As the buyer got more involved with the business, he realized her main function was HR. It soon became evident he expected more productivity from her. She didn't want to work any harder, and she left. She was replaced by a salesperson, which was what the company needed.

Vendors and Their Terms

A common worry from buyers is when the vendors don't have contracts, yet many (most) don't. Again, the vendor doesn't want to lose a good customer. So often it comes down to the question of whether the vendor will extend the same credit terms to the buyer as the seller has. This is less of an issue when one solid company is buying another. Don't overlook it, but it's surely not the top issue.

Growth and Integration

The best for last! This is the top concern for most buyers. First, is the firm's competitive advantage strong enough to enable growth? Second, will the two firms integrate operations and culture well enough to achieve that growth?

As one client wrote to me, "This is why they call it due diligence." While there's financial diligence to pick apart the numbers, just as important is the investigation of all the other aspects of the business to get an understanding of the future possibilities.

After all, this is why you're making an acquisition. No matter what the "other" reasons, if there's no growth or the cultures don't mesh, why do a deal?

What You Buy and What You Don't

These are the things keeping buyers up at night. While not as worrisome as declining sales, shrinking margins, or the big customer leaving, these things can distract from the transition, operations, and growth. Not too much explanation here, as they're self-evident.

- Warranties—if warranties are part of the business, the buyer wonders what's out there.
- Overdue raises—even worse was the seller who announced the sale and told the employees they were all due raises (from the buyer, of course).
- Gift cards—a lot more businesses besides retail and restaurants offer gift cards these days. What's out there? Are they tracked? Are they recorded properly? A lot of owners don't want the accounting hassle, so they simply record them as immediate sales. As a buyer, you hope there's a good list of what's outstanding so you're not providing goods you're not being paid for.

- Litigation—sometimes it's easy to find, but future litigation may be lurking around the corner, and often it's not. It may be the seller's responsibility, but it's one heck of a distraction.
- Unexpected change—all buyers worry about anything changing. It's a natural tendency.
- Tax problems—tax problems transcend an ownership change, and while it will be handled in the contract, it's sure not fun.
- Software licenses—are they legal, current, paid for? It's tougher to get black-market software than it used to be, but I've seen high five-figure postsale expenses because of unlicensed software.
- Nondocumented employees—this is always a big one and self-explanatory.
- Under market deals—these include under market rent, a brother-in-law as a supplier, and discount programs the buyer can't get (disabled veteran program, women/minority business).
- Minority business enterprise—if the seller has this and gets jobs you can't get, it can come back to haunt you.
- Overdue capital expenditures—you should ask, "When do I have to replace it, how much will it cost, and why didn't you do it?"
- Obsolete inventory—of course it will sell; just because we've had it nine years doesn't mean it's not good.
- Surprises—surprises are good for parties but not for buy-sell deals, unless the seller announces the day before closing a huge, unexpected order was just received.

Seller Emotions

If you think your emotions will be up and down like a roller coaster, multiply it to get to what the seller is going (to go) through. Seller remorse can manifest itself in many ways, and it starts with the first of four nondeal-related emotional subjects.

1. It's my "baby" I'm selling. Yes, often it is the seller's baby, and perhaps you feel the same way about your business. But babies

grow up, and like a good parent, a good owner will realize when it's time to let go, especially to a good buyer. One of my clients wanted a very small business for a proprietary product, which my client's firm used. Unfortunately, the seller thought his firm was the salvation for Western civilization. While we weren't far apart on price, he wanted to stay on for three years to make sure the buyer did things "the right way" with his product.

2. What does the owner's spouse think of him selling the business? Is she scared to have him around 24-7, and is she letting him know that? That's why it's so important (and what I recommend as part of the exit planning process) for the seller to have a plan for him next great adventure in life.

3. Then there's the aspect of money. Is it enough for what's next? I will tell you there's usually a lot more seller angst on smaller deals versus larger deals. On small deals, the seller is counting every dime, worrying about every little bit of working capital, etc.

4. And then there's the topic of "Why are you asking all these questions?" A lot of owners think their business is so special they can't understand why a buyer needs to ask so many questions. Plus, there's the issue of buyers asking the same question more than once. Sometimes it's because the diligence process is like taking a drink from a fire hose; there's a ton of information. Other times, the buyer will ask the question twice to see if the answer is the same.

The seller is going through a lot, hasn't done it before, and there's a 90 percent chance he hasn't done much, if any, preparation. Just like you're making a leap of faith, so is he. He's leaving his daily comfort zone, and the unknown can be scary. When both sides understand the other party has emotions at play, it goes a lot smoother.

Why They Made an Acquisition

Rick Locke is the owner of Windows Doors & More Inc. in Seattle, Washington (www.windowshowroom.com). When he bought WD&M in

2001, he used his varied business management experiences to take full responsibility for the strategy, decisions, and success of the company. He'd had lots of opportunities to provide input but was never the ultimate decision-maker, and he always felt his personal financial success was limited based on being an employee. For his second acquisition, of a similar company doing business in Montana and Idaho, he says, "Now, as a business owner (with some positive experiences and outcomes behind me), I see the opportunity to scale, leverage, and compound the assets I've developed both personally and with the business through acquisition." His key motivators are the following:

- Geographic diversification
- Market segment diversification
- Access to suppliers
- Access to key best practices
- Intellectual property
- Access to key people
- Ability to develop economies of scale through use of resources as well as volume-based purchasing power (that applies to everything from products to fees for 401(k) plans)

During his initial search, he loved seeing the different types of businesses and understanding how they made (or didn't make) money. One of his lines has always been "business is business," and he now believes that. However, at a microlevel, the differences between businesses are vast and extraordinary. He found it fascinating to deep dive on a number of businesses, learning lessons from every one of them, which he's applying now. The same applied as he evaluated his second acquisition firm; they did some things differently, and better, than he did.

His top tip is, "It's always about people. While you are buying capabilities, infrastructure, supply chain, a balance sheet, and customers, you are really buying people. There need to be a few key players who make the business what it is (other than the seller), and you need to recognize that early and develop their trust and loyalty."

One last comment about Rick and his deals. On the second one, when his CPA firm told him he wasn't negotiating hard enough, he said, "I should also tell you that when I bought Windows, Doors, and More my accountants told me I was crazy then too!" It is all about making a manageable leap of faith.

CHAPTER 8

IT'S WORTH WHAT? ARE YOU KIDDING?

I 've heard many variations of this title when delivering assessments of value to business buyers and owners. Once, within a two-week span, I heard the following from two owners.

- "It's worth that much? I had no idea."
- "My business has to be worth at least one-third more than this."

Beauty is truly in the eye of the beholder. There are tons of books on business valuation, most of them written for experts and service providers and most aimed at the middle-market and public-company market. They are way too technical for the small- to midsized-company niche.

Let's concentrate on the practical side of what's it worth, including the following:

- The seller's motivation
- The basics
- Some methodologies (formulas)
- The nonfinancial factors and their importance
- Myths of business valuation
- Why a business may be worth less (or more) than one might think

The Basics of Valuation

As per chapter 3, the more catastrophic a personal event, the more urgency on the part of the seller. The seller's motivation doesn't affect value, but it does affect price. So let's discuss value influencers.

The basics help determine what it's worth. No matter what anybody says, whether a certified valuation expert or a person off the street, there are some basic facts of life when it comes to what a small to midsize business is worth. Here are nine of them, with a tenth being the previously mentioned working capital adjustor. The last one is ever-present, causes the most consternation, and creates the most discussion.

But before we get to them, realize this: the business is worth what the seller and you agree on as a price. It doesn't matter if the company is profitable or not, how much sweat equity the seller feels he has, how long the firm's been in business, what a valuation says, the amount of debt, or anything else. None of them matter, other than to play a part in arriving at the agreed-upon price.

What's the Multiple?

I am asked all the time, "What's the multiple for this business (or industry)?" (multiple of profit, like a public company's price-earnings ratio). My answer is always the same, "I don't know, but if we can talk about the business a bit, I can give you a general range." You see, too many people think there are set formulas that make it simple. To steal from the next section on nonfinancial factors, let me ask, "Which is riskier—a business with 80 percent of their sales to three customers or a similar business with 80 percent of their sales to 117 customers?" Obviously, the latter has less customer risk. And there are many issues like this affecting the value. It's these factors that determine the multiple, not some preset, one-size-fits-all formula.

Risk versus Reward

The example in the previous paragraph brings up what might be the main issue when valuation is integrated with price. One buyer may see great risk in a certain company trait while another sees it as opportunity. A buyer commented the company didn't have a CRM system and didn't track customer attrition or why they left. My question was, "Is that a risk to you or opportunity?" He concluded it was an opportunity.

A buyer will pay more (than another buyer, than a valuation report states, etc.) if she feels she can quickly and dramatically scale the business. This could be based on her experience, risk tolerance, or some another factor. Risk versus reward is not a true valuation factor, but it is a deal factor, and the ultimate goal is to get the deal done.

When Both Parties Win

Often sellers think another company in their industry will pay more than an individual buyer or a company in a different industry. Sometimes it's true; sometimes it isn't. In this case, it was true. The buyer determined he didn't have to replace the owners' salaries and could eliminate the outside marketing firm with his people, and his current staff plus one person could handle the additional administration, thus eliminating three people. The added cash flow allowed him to pay double what someone would have paid had he kept the operation intact, and he still got a 25 percent ROI.

Ranges of Value

Fact—there are generally accepted ranges of value for businesses of a certain size. A microbusiness, like a dry cleaner or deli, is not going to get the same multiple as a $5 million business, which is not going to get the same multiple as a $25 million business, all other factors being equal. While this transcends industries for the most part, there are always exceptions.

In 2017–18 (and the few years prior), aerospace manufacturing businesses are getting higher multiples than other, similarly sized, manufacturing businesses. A manufacturing business with a proprietary product will usually get a higher multiple than a machine shop. For the most part, realize what you pay for something will fall in a certain range. Where it falls in that range is a function of all the other factors, including the nonfinancial factors, motivations, expectations, and risk tolerance.

Real Multiples

As I write this, according to the *Wall Street Journal*, the current PE ratio for the S&P 500 is 25.89. For a recent assignment, I researched this subject for private businesses, and the PE ratio for middle-market companies is just under 7× (as per GF Data, provided by my friend John O'Dore with Chinook Capital Advisors, a middle-market M&A firm in Kirkland, Washington) and just under 4× for small businesses, $1–15 million in sales (as per PeerComps, a database I subscribe to, which is information from closed SBA business-acquisition loans). For reference, a check of major bank PE ratios shows they are at about 15. An appraiser using 15× instead of 4–7× not only inflates the value but also commits fraud.

This confirms something I've been saying for years; there is a standard range in which businesses sell. For small businesses, it's three to five times profit (after fair market owner compensation). In the PeerComps data (over nine thousand business-acquisition loans), the coefficient of variance was just over 25 percent.

This means the range of multiples, the average of which is 4×, was just over one point above and one point below, or about 3–5×. There is a wide range because of the difference, firm to firm, of the nonfinancial factors, including customer concentration, management quality, dependency on the owner, and more. An average of 4× doesn't mean they all sell at this multiple; some are higher and some lower. But it also doesn't mean a small business will sell for 7× or a middle-market business will sell for 15×

(without very special mitigating factors, as there are always rare exceptions).

Going back a few years (more than a few), from the TV show *Hill Street Blues*, as Sergeant Esterhaus would say, "Hey, let's be careful out there."

The Logical Buyer

To a seller, selling to the right person is often much more important than getting the maximum price. Sellers are as human as you and me. They want to see the employees keep their jobs and thrive, the customers be taken care of, and their legacy preserved. I've given examples of where the seller took a lower price than she could have received or lower than another offer, because the buyer was the "right person."

Common Methodologies

IRS ruling 59–60 defines "fair market value, in effect, as the price at which the property would change hands between a willing buyer and a willing seller when the former is not under any compulsion to buy and the latter is not under any compulsion to sell, both parties having reasonable knowledge of relevant facts."

Well, the IRS should have said "hypothetical" buyer or hypothetical situation. Because never will the buyer and seller know the same things, perceive them the same way, or have the same motivations to do a deal now versus maybe next year.

This ruling covers some valuation methodologies, some of which are usually appropriate and some of which aren't. In the early twenty-first century, the SBA came out with their list of approved methodologies (I'm not sure if they still adhere to that list, but they now require appraisers to have a certification if they are to be approved to do valuations on SBA transactions).

The ruling also lists nine methodologies. However, most aren't applicable to the buy-sell world. For example, a profitable company isn't going to sell for book value (one of the methodologies), as all involved hope there are huge profits that create goodwill.

Another methodology not useful other than for a commonsense double check is the market method (i.e., comparable sales). This is not like real estate, where all transactions are recorded. As in the previous story, it's a wide range. Plus, small business is niche business, so it's unlikely you'll find enough transactions for exactly what a company does. So we tend to look at industries in general.

We'll cover the three most appropriate valuation methodologies a little later.

The Balance Sheet

A very wise man and incredible operator once told me how he learned the importance of the balance sheet only when evaluating acquisition candidates. How true. Often, I look at the balance sheet first, before the income statement. And yet, I know many people selling businesses don't understand the balance sheet or its importance. It can tell you about cash flow, asset upkeep, asset replacement (is the seller bleeding the cash from the company?), and more. Don't ignore it.

Terms

It's what you get, what you keep, and when you get it. An all-cash requirement often means a lower price, statistics say a discount of up to 30 percent or more. For deals qualifying for an SBA-guaranteed (to the bank) loan, most sellers are getting almost all in cash, without any huge discount. It's because the seller's advisors know bank policies, and the bankers get paid based on the volume of their loans, so they want to lend the maximum, which is, as I write this, 90 percent of the price (effective in 2018).

Taxes

To any seller, it's what they receive after closing costs and especially taxes. Most of the seller's proceeds should be capital gains. Some traps in which the seller doesn't want to be snared include the following:

- Assets valued above book value—CPAs call these "hot assets," as there will be depreciation recapture, and that amount is taxed as ordinary income
- A large allocation to the noncompete agreement, as this is ordinary income to the seller (and goodwill to the buyer)
- An allocation to transition training, again ordinary income to the seller (and in this case immediately deductible to the buyer)

You Can't Make This Up

We received an asset allocation from the seller's CPA that included a $500,000 amount for the noncompete agreement. I called him and asked, "Are you sure you want to do that to your client?" He asked what I meant. I said it was $500,000 of ordinary not capital gains taxation to his client. He replied that it was goodwill, to which I said, "I won't argue. We'll accept it, but you should research it." A call back later that day came with some embarrassment and a big thank-you. We reduced the noncompete to $10,000 but added a $50,000 training allocation, which the buyer got to deduct his first year.

Adjustments, Assumptions, and Add-backs

This is an ever-present contentious issue between buyer, seller, and intermediary. The seller wants to get a higher price, and the intermediary wants to get a higher commission or simply get the listing. So the financials are manipulated to show more profit than there really is and thus a higher price. In many cases, these actions are fraudulent (or they deceive the buyer, who will pay the ultimate penalty of lower-than-expected profits).

Adjustments are when the buyer is told expenses can be adjusted (reduced) in the future. For example (the following are true), the $250,000 of pension contributions can be cut in half, so that's really profit. Bonuses are discretionary, even though they've been given for the last fifteen years, or sales commissions can be reduced from 12 to 10 percent. As a buyer, isn't that exactly what you want to do in your first one hundred days—cut compensation and benefits? Wow, what a way to build respect and rapport with your employees!

Assumptions are also used to inflate earnings. I've seen the following:

- Projections showing the gross margin higher than they've ever been.
- Sellers and intermediaries telling the buyer he can lease less or cheaper space somewhere else, and that's more profit (forget the existing lease or the moving costs).
- Projections showing growth rates higher than ever experienced.
- The showing of future staff reductions (coupled with solid growth projections); in one case, this was presented after the seller said the reason for selling was "I'm tired of working too many seventy-to-eighty-hour weeks."

These are real-life examples and, as you can surmise, similar to sleight-of-hand tricks.

Add-backs are the mainstay of profit-inflating techniques. What add-backs are saying is this: "We wrote off a lot of expenses on our taxes that really aren't related to the business (therefore we've mislead the IRS)." Now, some things are legitimate. A corporation can hold their annual meeting in Hawaii in January and write it off. It isn't illegal, but it isn't a necessary business expense either. Other add-backs border on the ridiculous. Here are some from recent deals that didn't happen, one reason being the sellers wanted the price based on the following.

- Writing off (personal) Costco bills for all members of this multi-generational business

- Deducting gas, repairs, insurance, and more on all family members' (personal) vehicles
- Receiving the annual rebate from their distributor personally, not to the company (think that got reported on their 1040?)
- Writing off bills for (supposed) personal travel, meals, and the like (at such a high amount, it meant that nobody did much work between trips and other entertainment)

This list doesn't even include the most common add-backs: the owner's salary, benefits, and perks. This allows the seller or broker to use the term "seller's discretionary income (SDE)." Some business brokers actually believe the owner's salary is discretionary. I'm guessing they also believe mortgage payments are discretionary. Don't fall for this stuff; your bank won't.

It Really Happens

I would be remiss not to mention Kurt (not his real name) and his little black book. It was a detailed listing of all the personal expenses he deducted as business expenses. I thought I'd seen and heard just about everything when it comes to deducting personal expenses but not like the little book he kept in his pocket.

I've seen expenses from the liquor store, Costco, the toy train store, Best Buy, the cigar store, spouses' cars, family cars, family salaries (for people not working at the company), the weekly grocery bill, vacations, home remodels, and more. I once wrote a newsletter about an article in the *Minneapolis Star-Tribune* about a Twin Cities business owner who was put in jail for not reporting income and writing off things that made the previous list seem tame.

I've had owners brag about the cash they skim, and one owner even asked me, being dead serious, if I wanted to see the real books or the books he shows the IRS.

Many years ago, a CPA told me he fired a client because of this type of manipulation (CPAs can lose their license if they knowingly sign a fraudulent tax return). He said he told his client that because the client owned a well-known and successful restaurant, lived in one of the nicest neighborhoods in town, and drove an exotic car he, the CPA, couldn't sign his tax return showing he made a minuscule amount of money.

To balance this, there are legitimate add-backs to profit that could include the following:

- Life insurance on the seller (although not tax deductible unless she wants to pay income tax on the proceeds).
- Rent in excess of market (when the seller owns the building and will lease it for the lower market rate).
- Adjustments to depreciation with the recent high levels of section 179 deductions (as long as anticipated capital expenditures are factored in).
- Owner compensation to market rate (this could make profit higher or lower depending on how the seller pays herself).

AAA in the world of driving a car is cheap "insurance." And it truly can save the day. (Excessive) AAA in the buy-sell world is akin to "putting lipstick on a pig." You can dress the business up, but if it takes adjustments, assumptions, and add-backs to make the deal work, it's the wrong deal. If it's (sorry for all the clichés) "the icing on the cake" that makes the deal great instead of just good, you can probably live with it.

How Many Names Can You Have for Profit?

Profit, EBITDA, SDE, ODI, recast income, free cash flow, and other terms bounce around the buy-sell industry like a racquetball in a fast-paced game. What's worse is that these terms are often defined differently. Let's look at them, what they really mean, and how to apply them. Because no matter how a valuation methodology is applied, it comes down to a return on investment (ROI), and using one term versus another can create drastically different results.

- **Profit**

  It would be easier if businesses operated to maximize income instead of paying less in taxes. We'd get a truer picture of the income viability of a company. Small business reporting is not like public company reporting, where the public company wants to show maximum income to encourage their stock price to increase. For this reason, the profit figure on the income statement or the tax return is rarely valid.

- **Adjusted or Recast Profit**

  As per the previous section on AAA, this is what you will see. It allows a buyer and a lender to know what the buyer's available cash will be. This can be a very valid figure; just be careful of the traps.

- **EBITDA**

  The acronym stands for earnings before interest, taxes, depreciation, and amortization. This is supposed to give an indication of true cash flow because, in theory, depreciation and amortization are noncash expenses, and interest is included because a buyer may have different financing than the current owner. However, EBITDA doesn't make allowances for needed assets or the cost of working capital, which for many businesses is a critical, needed expense. As with adjusted profit, you must allow for a fair market salary for the job of the owner. This is a corporate term, and you don't see public companies adjust and add back management salaries to profits.

Tip—watch out for EBITDA (see more later in the section "Myths, Misnomers, and Truths"). For fun, Google "EBITDA and Warren Buffett." Here are a couple of choice quotes from Mr. Buffett or his longtime business partner, Charlie Munger, on the use of this term.

Depreciation is the worst kind of expense: You buy an asset first and then pay a deduction, and you don't get the tax benefit until you start making money.[2]

References to EBITDA make us shudder—does management think the tooth fairy pays for capital expenditures?[3]

Buffett's longtime business partner, Charlie Munger, expressed Berkshire Hathaway's position on this particular formula best: "I think that, every time you see the word "EBITDA," you should substitute the word 'bullshit' earnings."[4]

- **Seller's Discretionary Earnings**
  Also called owner's discretionary income (ODI), this is often EBITDA plus owner's salary, benefits, perks, and anything else they can add back. The theory is that all money to an owner is discretionary, and it's the owner's decision if he or she takes a salary, uses the money to grow the business, or pays acquisition debt. As mentioned previously, for most owners and buyers, a salary to support their personal life is not discretionary. An appraiser (and banker) will always allow for a fair market salary. In my opinion, not only is this somewhat fraudulent, but also this term loses any of its limited effectiveness once a business's adjusted profit plus salary gets to $500,000.
- **Free Cash Flow**
  In simple terms, take EBITDA (including the adjusted profit figure that allows for a fair market owner salary) and deduct anticipated capital expenditures and operating interest (not acquisition interest). This is a figure private equity groups and similar-type buyers often zero in on, especially in these days of complicated and changing accelerated depreciation schedules. It also gives a seller credit for recent capital expenditures that will reduce the buyer's need for capital expenditures.

Tip: Understand the Difference between S and C Corporations

A buyer reviewed a company's tax returns and said, "I like the business, but it's not making any money." The company was structured as a C corporation; the owner took a salary of about $750,000, which left only $50,000–100,000 on the net income line. Adjusting for a fair market salary gave a true adjusted profit figure in the $650,000–700,000 range.

Of course, I've seen buyers get excited when they first look at an S corporation's tax return and see an inflated net income line because the owner was taking a salary of only $50,000.

Multiples

These definitions are important to understand because, as previously stated, it all comes down to ROI. Your banker, appraiser, and you will all be concerned with the factor used as a multiple of earnings. The following example shows the differences, which are explained after the chart.

For this example, let's assume the company does about $5 million in sales, reports 10 percent profit before adjustments, and has a solid asset base (that needs regular upgrading). For this example, we are assuming there are no serious red flags, like high customer concentration, a tenuous lease that may require huge moving costs, or market factors that will negatively affect the industry.

Also, I'm assuming this is a manufacturing, distribution, or service business because retail and restaurant businesses have some additional factors, and their multiple of earnings is often lower because of the higher (perceived) risk associated with those business types.

	Profit	EBITDA	SDE	Free cash flow
Reported profit	$500,000	$500,000	$500,000	$500,000
Adjustments	$100,000	$100,000	$100,000	$100,000
Depreciation		$100,000	$100,000	$100,000
Operating interest		$50,000	$50,000	$50,000
Owner salary			$150,000	
Capital expenditures				-$50,000
Operating interest				-$50,000
NET	$600,000	$750,000	$900,000	$650,000

- **Profit**

  Buyers for businesses in this size range typically want a 20–25 percent ROI, which means a multiple of four to five. This gives us a price range of $2.4–3 million with a $2.7 million midpoint.

- **EBITDA**

  A $5 million business is between a three to four multiple. This gives us a price range of $2.2–3 million with a $2.6 million midpoint.

- **SDE**

  Your first inclination might be to want to use SDE, because it's a much higher number than the others. Of course, the generally accepted range of multiples is lower. Around the year 2000, I was being recruited to join a prominent Seattle business brokerage firm. Their typical deals were from $1 to $5 million in price, and they had a great reputation. One thing that stuck out to me was that in their weekly meetings, when discussing possible listings (of only profitable companies), they always used a range of two to three times when discussing SDE. The potential listing agent usually argued for the high end of the range, and the other agents gave reasons why that wasn't realistic (they actually used traditional valuation methodologies; SDE factors were for initial discussion only). Using this range, we get a price range of $1.8–2.7 million and a midpoint of $2.25 million.

- **Free Cash Flow**

  You'll find free cash-flow multiples to be similar to profit multiples, and they grow as companies get to $10 million in sales and above. In this example, we get a price range of $2.6–3.2 million and a midpoint of $2.9 million.

	Profit	EBITDA	SDE	Free cash flow
Mid-point value	$2,700,000	$2,600,000	2,250,000	$2,900,000

You can see why I feel SDE loses importance as a business grows. The owner's salary becomes less relevant compared to the lower multiple range. The other methodologies are in a pretty tight range, and then the influences become, as always, the nonfinancial factors, terms, relationships, and buyer and seller motivations.

I can tell you that some business brokers would read this and immediately argue that the range of multiples, the calculations, or other factors all give too low a value. At the same time, buyer representatives, accountants, and others would tell me that this is too optimistic.

As with any guidelines, use them only as such—a guideline. The previous list is simplistic and is presented to make a point. That point is that there are different ways to calculate earnings and different multiples for those methods. Buyers of $5 million businesses want a 20–25 percent ROI; buyers of $15 million or $50 million businesses will lower it to perhaps a 15 percent ROI. There's enough evidence and history to show these are viable ranges, and these are the ranges necessary to allow for the risk of a small business (versus the risks a large public company faces and can handle).

Story: If They Love You, the Price Is Great

The seller gave us the asking price, and after the meeting, the buyer and I looked at each other and simultaneously said, "What should we negotiate?" You see, the price was more than fair, so we didn't want to disrupt the deal. We negotiated part of the seller financing and a few conditions, and that was it. It's too bad they're not all that easy.

Determine the True Cash Flow

This is where the fun begins. It's rare to find a small business that has a tax return or income statement that accurately reflects the true profit of the company. One part of the reason is that there are tax techniques, such as accelerated depreciation and amortization of goodwill (if they purchased the company and are still writing off the goodwill). The other big reason is that owners funnel nonbusiness expenses through the company.

Business owners should approach their bottom line, at least for three to five years prior to selling, as if they are in a contest to have the most profit and pay the most tax. However, that's tough for most owners. They either have a great aversion to paying taxes, or their CPA takes it as his or her mission to reduce the client's taxable income by any means possible.

It is considered fraud not to report income and to deduct personal expenses through the business. I don't recommend it, but it happens, and that is one reason it is common to "recast" or adjust the income statement to show the true profit and cash flow the buyer should expect.

The following chart is a simple tool to help you calculate your profit or cash flow that will be available. Most of the categories are self-explanatory, but let's review some of them. First, realize that in an S corporation, the owner often takes a low salary and high distribution, and in a C corporation, it is the opposite. Therefore, we add back owner compensation to net income and deduct the fair market salary for the job being performed by the owner.

Category	2 Years Prior	Last Year
Net Income		
Owner salary		
Owner salary tax burden		
Excessive owner benefits (life insurance, etc.)		
Travel & Entertainment (not essential)		
Owner auto (not essential)		
Depreciation adjustment		
Amortization (of Goodwill)		
Interest (not continuing post-sale)		
Rent adjustment (that you over or under pay yourself for rent)		
Other		
Other		
Total		
Less: Fair market owner salary		
Less: Fair market owner tax burden		
Less: Anticipated capital expenditures		
Less: Other		
Total adjusted net profit/free cash flow		

- **Excessive Owner Benefits**

  If the seller has life insurance, deferred compensation, or a pension plan weighted in his favor, you can add these back to income. Do not add back standard medical benefits, similar to what all employees get, and what you will have to pay for if you're replacing the seller with somebody else.

- **Nonessential Expenses**

  Do they deduct their car, yet use it only to commute? Or perhaps the spouse's or kids' cars? What about that annual board meeting in Hawaii in January? These are not expenses essential to running the business.

- **Depreciation**

  Work with your CPA to get a cost for anticipated capital expenditures and asset usage expense, which is really what depreciation is, other than all the acceleration techniques.

- **Interest and Rent**

  If there's an acquisition loan, you should add back to income the interest on it. Realize with a line of credit, you might have an operating interest expense also, so factor that cost into your calculations. Rent is adjusted only if the seller owns the building and is charging himself under- or overmarket rent.

There are too many businesses that have become "lifestyle" businesses for the owner. There's a blending of the personal and business checkbooks. Some CPAs are aggressive and tell their clients to write off anything and everything. Others are incredibly conservative and will question why your annual board meeting wasn't at your office.

Banks are increasingly suspicious when there's a long list of add-backs of personal expenses. Many bankers will discount these and thus reduce the cash flow they will use to calculate debt-coverage ratios.

Comparable Sales

Historical sales information (i.e., comparable sales) is a little bit like the Bible. There is one Bible and many different interpretations. The same can be said for the interpretation of done-deal benchmarks. If a business is below average, the owner or selling team will point to average multiples as a way to increase the price.

We can learn a lot from history. Of course, we should pay attention and allow for other factors.

As mentioned, consider your use of average selling prices. I've had discussions with many people about the validity of (historical) average selling prices. Rarely will a business be average. Don't get caught in the trap of using averages as gospel.

Toby Tatum, certified business appraiser and the author of *Transaction Patterns*, wrote to my "Partner" On-Call Network associate Ted Leverette and said, "Using a 3x multiple of seller's discretionary earnings for the vast majority of businesses represented in the Bizcomps database will tend to yield a value conclusion that is approximately double the correct amount." Or a small percentage of good businesses are raising the average price of all the others. So be careful.

Use Common Sense with Comparable Information

There weren't enough historical sales for the distribution company's SIC (standard industrial classification) code, so we looked at distribution companies in general, at a size range that straddled this firm's size and eliminated all firms losing money. We noted the ratio of price to earnings (the multiple) and, just as important, the ratio of earnings to revenues.

The firm had earnings 20 percent greater than the average—for example, if the average was 15 percent, then this firm had 18 percent earning. Our assumption became that this firm was an above-average firm, and it justified the price should be above average. This is just one way to use comparable sales information.

My advice to buyers and sellers is not to get hung up on comparable sales information. This is not like real estate, where it's a regulated market. Submissions to most of the databases are voluntary (unlike tax records), and there are no double checks on the information submitted (other than Peer Comps, the SBA loan database, which is real information). This information is really a guideline or rule of thumb and should be used accordingly.

We also don't know exactly what was included in the reported information. If two owners sell for five times profit and one keeps all the working capital and the other includes it in the deal, we have vastly different sales that are reported with the same price-to-earnings ratio. Or what if one deal included real estate and the other didn't?

Real-Life Numbers

As mentioned, I subscribe to a service called PeerComps, which is a database of done deals financed with SBA loans. For years, I have said the typical range for small business values (and prices) is three to five times profit (about the same for EBITDA in most cases). In a study of done deals of companies with sales of $1–20 million (no agriculture, mining, utilities, insurance, or real estate), the average multiple of EBITDA was 3.85 with a coefficient of variance of 0.38. This means the standard range was about 2.5–5.5 times. FYI, the average EBITDA percentage of revenue was 16.62 percent, and the numbers hardly varied if it was all businesses or larger firms for those with sales of $10–20 million.

Practical Small Business Valuation Methods
In my world, it comes down to the fact that there are three main methods, with comparable sales used as a sanity check. Research business valuations, and you'll find a lot of appraisers talking about how there's as much art as science to it (and they're right).

Capitalization of Earnings
For a small or midsized business, what are the most valid methodologies? Return on investment or capitalization of earnings is always at the top of the list. It's using a multiple of earnings. Any buyer (you, if you're growing by acquisition) wants a rate of return commensurate with the perceived risk of the business. Therefore, larger companies will sell for a higher multiple than smaller ones, all other factors being equal. There is less perceived risk.

In simple terms, the return on the investment determines the price of the business. If the buyer desires, or demands, a return of 20 percent based on historical earnings or on the perceived risks, then he or she will pay five times earnings for the business.

The IRS Method
As you might suppose, a method with the initials IRS in it will tend to lead to higher values, as the IRS often gets involved with gift and estate tax issues and wants a high value so there is more tax to collect. In simple terms (you can easily do an Internet search to get more detailed information on this), the ongoing cost of the company's assets is deducted from earnings, and a multiple is applied. This becomes the

value of the goodwill, and it is added to the value of the assets. Here's an example:

Earnings—$500,000
Assets—$400,000
Cost of funds—10 percent (or an annual cost of $40,000 for the use of these assets)
Goodwill ratings—4 (or 25 percent desired rate of return)

Profit	$500,000
Cost of assets	-$40,000
Net	$460,000
Multiple	4
Goodwill ($460,000X4)	$1,840,000
Value of assets	$400,000
Value of assets and goodwill	$2,240,000

You can see that the rate of return on this price is 22 percent or 12 percent less than the buyer's desired 25 percent return on investment. That's why it's stated that this method gives high values. The values become more skewed (higher) when there are high asset values and low-to-average profits, as the following example shows.

Example: Common Sense Says Watch Out for What Doesn't Make Sense

The firm being sold was a high-inventory business. In fact, the amount of their inventory was many times higher than similar firms because of overseas manufacturing and shipping, the number of product variables (size, color, style), and production lead times. Using the IRS valuation method gave a value so high that no buyer would pay it. The return on investment would be way too low for this $10 million (sales) company.

The fact was the company was getting a very poor return on assets, and its value was about the total value of the assets because of this. In this case, growth was the answer. At twice its size, the firm projected it would need the same inventory with a better inventory turn rate.

Discounted Future Cash Flow

Personally, I think buyers and sellers should be very careful of this method or any variation of it. It's often said that buyers buy because of potential and pay based on history. This method determines a price based on future, projected earnings. I'm not alone with these thoughts. The SBA will not allow a valuation that uses projections of any type. The value should be determined based on historical earnings.

Again, in simple terms, the projected earnings have a discount rate applied to them to create a present value of those earnings. This sounds fine in theory, but just imagine the situation if someone bought a company in 2007 based on all the rosy projections floating around. Nobody imagined the Great Recession. As a seller, you don't want to be dragged into a lawsuit because you sold based on projections that didn't come true (whether it's the buyer's fault, the economy, or anything else).

Real-Life Story: Watch Out for Agendas (Again)

A client showed me two valuations done on his firm. The first was from a national, road-show company that sold incredibly expensive valuation reports and was known for inflated values in those reports. The value was so high that this owner just laughed because he knew that, even in his wildest dreams, no buyer would pay that amount. They got these high values by basing them on projected earnings.

The second valuation was from a very reputable regional CPA firm. They used the same method (discounted future earnings) and added in a residual value. This means that they projected the buyer would sell the business in five years; they discounted to a net present value the price the buyer would receive and added it to the current value (based on projections). In other words, pay the seller now for what you will sell it for in the future. Their value was even higher than the national firm's value.

Again, the risk is a future lawsuit if those projections don't materialize. This client was smart enough to know that he wouldn't buy his own business for these inflated prices and no sane buyer would either.

Goodwill Ratings

I've used the term "goodwill" numerous times, so let's define it. In simple terms, goodwill is the difference between the value of the assets of the company and the company's value based on other valuation methods (the value created by profit). Every buyer, seller, and even banker should want a lot of goodwill. It means the company is getting a great ROI on its assets. Some bankers and unsophisticated buyers will call it "blue sky." Some bankers refer to it as an "air ball," meaning it might not have any value because it isn't collateral they can attach to. My feeling is that goodwill is valid; it's a number based on profits. Blue sky is on top of goodwill and a number based on unrealized potential.

The following is a standard form used by business appraisers to estimate the feelings of company owners or buyers on the goodwill of the firm. You can find it in many places (perhaps with some slight variations).

I instruct clients, "Rate your company or your target company and be honest. Give thought to each category listed below, and put down the number you feel is most representative of the company's status." *Ratings do not need to be whole numbers and can range from 0 to 6 (e.g., they could be 3.1, 4.7, 1.4, or 5.0).*

Give serious thought to your answers, and justify them. Question why you chose a particular number rather than a higher or lower one. For example, if a rating is a 4, why is it not 4.5 or 5, and why is it not 3.5 or 3?

Please provide a brief explanation of why you chose each rating. Be skeptical of any ratings at the 5 or 6 level. It is highly unusual for a business to be at a 5 or 6 in any of these areas. A score at this level means your firm is in the "best-of-the-best" category. Provide *proof* of why you're at this level.

Alternatively, if you give a rating of 1 or 2 in any category, please give a brief explanation of why you don't think you're up to speed in that area.

Risk Rating _____

0   Continuity of income is uncertain
3   Steady income likely
6   Growing income assured

Competitive Rating _____

0   Highly competitive in unstable market
3   Normal competitive conditions
6   Little competition in market, high cost of entry

Industry Rating _____

0   Declining industry
3   Industry growing faster than inflation
6   Dynamic industry, rapid growth likely

Company Rating _____

0   Recent start-up or not established
3   Well established with satisfactory environment
6   Long record of profitable operation and excellent reputation

Company Growth Rating _____

0   Business declining
3   Steady growth, slightly faster than inflation
6   Dynamic growth rate

Desirability Rating _____

0   No "prestige" status; rough, dirty, undesirable work
3   Respected type of business in good environment
6   Great demand by people desiring to own this type of business

Total Rating _____

These ratings serve two purposes. First, they give insight into the buyer's and the seller's feelings about the company, its future, and the risk involved. Second, in the IRS valuation method, the average of these ratings is often used along with a desired rate of return. For example, if the average is 4.3, it translates into a 23 percent desired ROI. Caveat—it is tough to use only the average rating when the instructions say that it's rare to have ratings of 5 or above.

Real-Life Story: Human Nature Gets in the Way Sometimes

The two owners, one buying the shares of the other, each filled out this rating form. The buyer's ratings averaged between 2 and 3. The selling partner's ratings were one 4 and five 6s.

Of course, both were wrong, and in this case, the buyer was closer to reality. For example, both buyer and seller told me that the industry was not growing very much, and their growth was at the expense of competitors. Yet the selling partner gave "industry rating" a 6, "dynamic industry, rapid growth likely." I think both of them were trying to influence me.

Nonfinancial Factors and Their Effect

At "Partner" On-Call Network, we use the acronym CELBS (customers, employees, landlord, banker, and suppliers) to represent all the nonfinancial factors of a business. Those pesky little behind-the-scenes things that let you know if the profits will continue and grow. Here are seven of the most common nonfinancial factors and some examples of how they can affect a valuation.

Customers

Everybody talks about customer concentration and for a good reason. But what about customer loyalty and pricing? Having to replace one-third of your customers every year will take a toll. Do your customers pay a fair price, or are they there because of the price?

Employees

Are they capable? Are they loyal? Do they have room to grow? Are they paid fairly? These are some of the questions you should be asking. You find the answers by discussing them with the seller, looking at job descriptions, looking at employee reviews, and, finally, interviewing the employees. But what does this really mean? If you like the company and are confident you can grow it, then your impression may not change; you'll just realize there are (staffing) changes to be made. Or you can leverage any shortcomings into your price negotiations. A lot depends on the company and your relationship with the seller.

Culture

This is perhaps the eight-hundred-pound gorilla of nonfinancial factors. And sometimes it's a tough one to decipher until you're in the business. But what exactly is culture in a small business? To me, it's the attitude of working together to a common goal (e.g., to deliver the best product possible, on time). Things do get in the way of this. It could be a disruptive employee, an authoritarian manager, poor leadership, or no respect for values. You get a handle on this by getting to know the seller, meeting the key people, and just noticing how they do things. For example, a client had "beer Friday" once a month, and it was looked forward to by most if not all of the staff.

No Lifestyle Businesses, Please

I've seen culture disrupt multiple deals, the most recent being when the owner of a midsized machine shop was interested in buying a small shop (to gain needed capacity). After meeting the owner and his son, observing the operations, and subcontracting a job to the target firm, he ended the deal. There was no respect for timeliness, extenuated by the selling firm missing the deadline on the buyer's job! The buyer got the (valid) impression the employees punched in at 7:30 a.m. and punched out at 4:00 p.m., and if the jobs weren't done, they'd get to them tomorrow. The buyer's philosophy was to deliver jobs on time, even if it meant overtime. He realized his culture would clash with the seller's, and he'd be replacing employees in a tight labor market.

Lease

The chances of getting a bank loan with a term longer than the term of the lease, with options, are slim. The bank doesn't want the buyer forced into moving partway through the loan, and you shouldn't want this either, even if it's seller financing. It's expensive and disruptive to move most businesses, and the added expense may affect your bank debt-coverage ratios. (Caveat—an office-based business, like software, training, or accounting—may not have the same requirements as a manufacturing, retail, or distribution one.)

Management Team

My favorite question to an owner is, "Can you go to New Zealand for three to four weeks and return with the company in the same or better shape?" Recently, a client proudly let me know he had just returned from a long trip to New Zealand, and the business was as good as ever. He was pretty proud of that. Depending on the size of the company, you want a solid management team (if, as in the previous story, you're buying capacity and line workers, it's not important). When growing by acquisition, look for talent in the areas where you are weakest.

Suppliers

Often vendor agreements must be redone, and the buyer must qualify for credit terms, which shouldn't be an issue. I know of a bank who did diligence on a customer's top vendor because they were concerned with vendor concentration and wanted to make sure the vendor was solid.

Technology/Productivity

In early 2017, I was at a presentation on the aerospace industry. One of the comments was "Boeing is laying off people, including engineers, and robotics was a major factor in some of the layoffs." Robots are cheap. Be careful. Expensive technology doesn't give advantages only to larger firms. What you're looking for is a company that is under-technologized. That's an opportunity to increase productivity. Keep in mind it could be machine technology, like robots, or human technology, say using your smarts and experience to improve operations and productivity.

Myths of Business Valuation

Here are seven myths and misnomers plus three truths (some have already been covered).

I'm special, so special. No matter what the owner thinks, the chances of the business being so special or different that normal guidelines and methodologies don't apply are slim to none. Business is business, and just like a CPA can do the taxes for almost all industries, the valuation techniques are also industry agnostic.

EBITDA is realistic. It bears repeating; it can be very misleading to base the valuation on EBITDA if it's an asset-heavy business, especially if you don't discount the cap rate or rate of return from the one you'd use if you applied it to free cash flow. Don't fall into the trap of ignoring anticipated capital expenditures.

Real-Life Incompetence

A business broker who didn't understand accounting basics kept telling me how accountants told him depreciation was a noncash expense and therefore (he believed it) could be added into profit. But at some point, cash leaves the company's account and goes to the supplier. My answer these days is simple: "What about the payments to the bank for the equipment loans? Are they noncash as well?"

Owner's compensation equals profit. This is one of the most abusive myths in business sales. (I hesitate to use the word "valuation.") You see this the most with very small companies where they need to pump up the bottom line. Remember, no bank or business appraiser will treat owner compensation as profit; they will plug in a number for fair market compensation for the job being done.

Size doesn't matter. This is another myth that bears repeating. No matter what the owner thinks, a $5 million company isn't going to get the same multiple as a $50 million or $500 million company. There's just more risk with a smaller business (usually dependencies of some sort).

Rules of thumb and guidelines are important. It's a myth because it's not one-size-fits-all, and you don't know what's included in the deals used to create the rule. A seller going to his club and bragging about selling for seven times EBITDA but failing to mention it included the real estate isn't giving an accurate portrayal of the deal. When it comes to generalities, be skeptical.

Annual sales equals price. Most buyers are buying profit and future profit potential. The only time for basing price on revenue is when a similar company only cares about the revenue stream because they know their costs (not the seller's costs) to deliver the product for that revenue. Otherwise, don't even think about it.

Rules of Thumb Are Usually Wrong

Years ago, a client said to me, "I think my business is worth $X." I asked why, and she said, "I've always heard your business is worth two times your annual revenues." So I gave her my standard answer, which is, "If a competitor down the street is the same size as you and running at breakeven while you're making 15 percent profit, do you think the businesses are worth the same?"

The multiple is all that matters. As previously written numerous times, the multiple is not a number you pick; it's a number derived from the analysis of the business and its risk factors—of course, normally within a range for that size company. Too many people just go to the upper or lower end of the range and want to plug in that number.

Of course, there are truths out there, and three top ones (besides profits drive value and the larger the profits, the higher the value) are the following:

There are acceptable ranges. As mentioned before, there are normal ranges of value (the multiple) based on the size of the company, industry, and other factors. Unless there are huge and numerous red flags or "for sure" accelerated growth, the value will fall within this range.

It's all about ROI versus risk. The risk you are willing to accept determines your hoped-for and projected return on investment. It's obvious, the higher the risk, the lower the ROI, and vice versa.

It's science and art. There are all kinds of numbers and formulas, some discussed here. The art part is knowing the market, the activity, the number of buyers and sellers, the financing availability, and more. I'm amazed at how often I'm correct when I tell clients what it will take to get a deal and it's in that range (whether it's my client or someone else doing the deal).

When You're Too Smart for Your Own Good

My client told me he knew how to value businesses; he'd done it before. He ran his formulas and spreadsheets and came up with this: "The business is worth $2.5 million." I had told him it would take $4–4.5 million to get the company. Sure enough, it sold for $4.4 million. You see, anyone can manipulate formulas to get a high or low value. Just start changing factors and assumptions. FYI, this company had profit of $1 million a year with solid recurring revenue. How my client got to $2.5 million is beyond me.

Why It's Worth Less (than the Seller Hopes)

Here's a summary of what we've been discussing: twenty reasons a business may be worth less than the seller thinks it's worth. Please note, it's written to the seller, not the buyer, as a primer for what to do to make the business more attractive to people like you (and so you can identify these things in your business). Note, we've already covered some of these reasons.

1. Dependency on owner—too many businesses suffer from the all-controlling owner who not only knows how to do everything but also insists on being part of everything. Don't let yourself be the bottleneck. A buyer may pass or offer a lower amount when he sees how big the shoes he must fill are.

2. Customer concentration—no buyer wants there to be a small number of key customers doing a disproportionate share of your volume. Diversify your customer base, and realize if you have a highly concentrated customer (or industry) base, you may be asked to include an erosion clause that lowers the price if a top customer leaves.

3. Financial statements and tax returns differ—there isn't much to say about this. Have good accounting systems, safeguards, and accurate statements. Don't rely on too many adjustments for the tax return or an overwhelming amount of add-backs (to profit).

4. Dependency on a key employee—a company recently had severe problems when their top salesperson left and took most of their accounts. This problem could manifest itself with a technical expert, machine operator, or office manager (who knows how everything in the firm works; see dependency on the owner above).

5. Poor lease or no lease available—you may think a month-to-month arrangement is great, as it offers flexibility. Buyers and banks think about how expensive it is to move. In fact, for other than a professional-type business (like consulting, accounting, or similar), your buyer won't get a bank loan for longer than the term of the lease,

including options. Too short a lease means too short a seller or bank loan and too high a payment to make the deal feasible.

6. Behind the curve on technology—while some people will think this is an advantage to a buyer to do things more efficiently, in reality, there is a cost to hardware, software, and implementation. Use the experience of your business to get technology up to speed, show increased efficiencies (and profits), and sell for a higher price.

7. Skimming cash—there isn't a CPA around who will let a buyer be convinced to pay a price based on unreported cash. First, you are cheating the IRS. Second, is it worse that you're skimming, or worse that you say you are but really aren't?

8. Too small—a business doing $2 million in sales will not get the same multiple of profits as a similar business doing $20 million. There are just more risk factors the smaller the business is. An issue that is a major disruption to a small firm is a minor hiccup to a larger firm.

9. You are blending too many personal expenses into the business—yes, there are advantages to paying for things with pretax dollars instead of after-tax dollars like employees have to. Carry it too far, and it's almost as bad as skimming. Bottom line, buyers and banks like to see profits. Show a lot of profit, pay some tax, and it will come back to you in multiples when you sell (and make it easier to sell and finance the business).

10. You have to work too hard in the business—buyers look for businesses they can work on, not work in. They may not have your passion for your product or service; instead, they have business skills to leverage what you've done. Get out of the business of doing things an employee could do.

11. Financing is hard to get—banks don't like your industry, your business, or acquisitions in your industry. If your industry requires a high level of industry experience, a buyer without that experience won't get an acquisition loan. However, you may get a higher price by financing more of the deal.

12. No business or marketing plan—while a plan may not directly reduce the value of your firm (other than via the fact that companies with a plan have significantly higher profits), a business and marketing plan may add to the price a buyer is willing to pay.

13. Poor or no management team—buyers like to manage and lead; they don't like to do. A poor team means a lower value.

14. Salary is not profit—an appraiser will want to know the fair market salary for the job of running the company. If you weren't there, you'd have to pay someone to be president, and that salary is not profit (by a long shot).

15. Saturation—this is often a function of franchising or low barriers to entry. Eventually, this leads to competition based on price, and it's hard to win in that situation.

16. Special skills or license needed—about two-thirds of all small businesses need an owner with general business skills and business common sense. Those are the types buyers like the most. If you have to be a PhD in an advanced scientific field to own the business, well, good luck finding someone with money who wants to own a business.

17. Vendor concentration—don't overlook this. The vendor(s) may not pull any tricks, but what happens if your sole source has problems or goes out of business?

18. Working capital needs—you pay your people this week. You pay your suppliers in thirty days and the rent and other overhead every month, and your customers pay you in ninety days. That's working capital, and that's why fast growth can be a problem. It takes cash to grow, and if you don't have access to enough cash, you've hit a bottleneck (see the first reason on this list).

19. You have a job, and it's not as CEO—in other words, you work in the business, not on the business. If the business can't survive if you're not on the shop floor, you aren't a manager; you're a working employee. This probably means growth is stagnant, as you have no plan, leadership, or management.

20. You've bled the business—every last cent goes into your take-home pay, and the assets need repair or replacement. This leads to lower profits. One owner was so cheap he wouldn't buy a new printer. After the sale, the buyer bought a new printer, the accounting department stopped having their systems freeze up when something printed, and their efficiency soared.

Learn from a Real-Life Example

Let me close the section on valuation with a story about a company on whose board of directors I serve. The company went through the process of an ESOP (employee stock ownership plan). It was the only way to give the founders liquidity without selling to a large corporation, which they didn't want to do for culture and legacy reasons.

ESOPs have the Department of Labor looking over everybody's shoulder to make sure the employees don't overpay. As part of the team interviewing trustees, I asked all of them, "What are the most common traps, and how do we avoid them?"

The universal answer was "the valuation," and they emphasized three points.

- Projections—you know I'm not a big believer in relying on projections (I have a video podcast titled "Projections Are Meaningless"); they are important with ESOPs. The appraiser must not only use projections but also compare past projections with reality. Any growth rates must be provable. A good request to make when presented with projections is this: "Let me see your last five years of projections."
- Comparable sales—a big issue is the use of public company comparable sales (the price-earnings ratio the same as the multiple) for middle-market companies and middle-market multiples for midsized firms (what I consider small businesses usually aren't large enough to do an ESOP, as

it's very expensive). The old cliché apples to apples is very apropos here.

- Methodologies—problems include improper use of standard valuation methodologies. Using public company price-earnings ratios is one improper technique. Another would be adjusting the goodwill rating factors used in the IRS method. Changing the standard 1-to-6 scale to a 1-to-10 scale makes the same business, rated at 70 percent of maximum, and have a multiple of 7, or about 15 percent ROI, from 4.2—about a 23 percent ROI. We could cover errors such as these for any valuation methodology.

These are simple examples with the point being if you approach it as an ESOP trustee would, you won't fall into traps.

Why They Made an Acquisition

Kevin Katona and Steve Duffield own Daco Inc. in Kent, Washington (www.dacocorp.com), a distributor of material-handling supplies and packaging as well as now designing and installing rack systems, as a result of a recent acquisition.

Kevin shared the primary reason he likes making an acquisition is because growth creates stability, and any swings seem to be less pronounced. He gave me two examples of this. First, when you have five people and lose one, it's a huge deal, but when you have fifty employees and lose one, it's no big deal. Second, because salespeople have their own cycles, with more people, these cycles mitigate each other, so the revenue flow is less erratic.

When they bought Applied Handling, they gained another area of expertise—racks and systems. They were able to offer this service to current customers and their product line to Applied Handling's customers. A bonus was they found they could get into accounts (with racks) they couldn't previously get into (with packaging).

Kevin's top tip is to pay attention to the details in all areas. He said they didn't do this as they put the two sales teams together, and it created competition instead of the desired collaboration. This was especially true with common customers. He wished they had "drawn the line in the sand" sooner. This is a good lesson on why a detailed transition plan is important.

CHAPTER 9

NO SURPRISES, PLEASE

Y ou're hungry for information, details, knowledge about the intricacies of the company, and more. Yet, if you rush the process, there's a great chance you'll lose the deal. "Go slow to go fast" is something I learned many years ago from my friend Ted Leverette. Go too fast and you'll raise the seller's skeptical antenna.

Remember the earlier story about the buyer who wanted the secret sauce and all the financial statements within twenty minutes of meeting a seller? It's not surprising he took *forever* to find a deal.

I have a simple five-step process for obtaining and using company information.

1. **Relationship**—as emphasized previously, this is a relationship game, and it starts from the first phone call, the purpose of which is to set up a time to meet in person. From there, use your natural charm to build rapport and trust. Remember, you're buying someone's "baby."

2. **Big-picture information**—start by getting three years of financial statements, tax returns, year-to-date statements, and the trailing twelve-month statements. Ask big-picture questions to uncover red flags. We use our seller's initial disclosure form, which is a couple of dozen yes/no, multi-subject questions designed to get

issues out in the open early. If you'd like a copy of it, e-mail me at john@johnmartinka.com.

3. **Offer**—make an offer based on the analysis of the above. Nicely let the seller know you need to know now if there are any issues threatening the future of the business. If you uncover them later, you'll be wondering what else is out there (and it may destroy the deal).

4. **Agreement**—sign a letter of intent based on the above.

5. **Due diligence**—this confirms what you've been told, does so in detail, and is no time for surprises.

Analysis versus Due Diligence

Here are three examples of the difference between analysis and due diligence.

Customers—during the analysis phase, you may get a customer list showing annual volume of sales to each but not the customers' names. During diligence, you'll get the names and the chance to (blindly) speak with them.

Financials—early on, you'll get the statements and tax returns. During diligence, expect to get a copy of the accounting software's file, state tax forms, and bank statements so you can get all the details you want.

Employees—analysis provides a list of people, an org chart, and an overview. After an agreement is reached, you'll get employee reviews, job descriptions, and a chance to meet and interview the people (at least the management staff and key people). The last item usually happens after the purchase and sale agreement is signed, with meeting the employees a final contingency.

Earlier, I discussed your team and its bandwidth for a search. The same applies for the diligence process, as it takes time and effort. Determine in advance who will lead and define roles. Given I'm primarily referring to small to midsized acquisitions (not middle market), the owner will probably lead the charge. The size of the management team determines how much and what will be delegated (without distracting too much from their day-to-day duties). And don't forget to use your outside advisors. Not too many words on this topic, but that doesn't mean it's not important. Don't get bogged down here and sabotage a deal because you haven't allocated enough time for this. When investment banks do buy side work it's often because their client doesn't have the management time to devote to the process.

What Am I Really Buying (Due Diligence)?

First, realize there are more due-diligence questions out there than you could ever ask (or want to ask). Just do an Internet search; you'll be overwhelmed.

Before we get to the questions and important topics, realize due diligence is twofold. It's finding things out about the company to make sure you're getting what you think you're getting. Just as important, it allows you to engage the seller in dialogue so you learn operating techniques and other intricacies about the business (before you take over). This is why you do it in person, not in writing.

I recommend the best list to start with is the one from your attorney (keeping in mind the seller's initial disclosure form I mentioned is your first diligence effort). It will have the *required* topics and should correspond with their list of schedules to the purchase and sale agreement (the schedules are the written statements by the seller about the business, which he is representing and warrantying are true and correct). Once you get this list from your attorney, go through it, and, with your attorney's input, determine which topics don't apply to your deal.

However, there's a lot more to understanding what you're buying than the items on the attorney's list. I don't try to "compete" with the attorney lists. Most of my questionnaires have softer questions and general areas of interest. I call my two primary lists "Master List and Questions" (which is in the appendix section) and "Nonfinancial Questions." Here's an example of the difference.

- On the master list, one question asks for the last three years of sales volume by customer—pretty general.
- On the nonfinancial question list, we ask, "When did you let down a customer, and how did you rectify it?" This is less data driven and gives more insight into how the company is run.

If you'd like a copy of my master list in Word or a copy of the nonfinancial questions, please e-mail me at john@johnmartinka.com.

I always get asked by owners what are the top things they can do to make their business more attractive to buyers. My standard answer—which is also in my book *If They Can Sell Pet Rocks, Why Can't You Sell Your Business (For What You Want)?*—is the top three areas are the following:

- Have solid financial systems and accurate financial statements.
- Show the company can grow; don't just say it has potential.
- Reduce dependencies, especially on the owner.

I have since added, based on current labor-market conditions, to show how you attract and retain top-quality talent.

Financial

Where most buyers start, and it's the right place to start, is the financial statements and tax returns. Just as important is the system, chart of accounts, and proper allocation of expenses (proper cost of goods allocation for example). When done right, the financial statements and tax returns at least look like they're from the same company.

As I previously mentioned, the balance sheet is just as important as the profit and loss statement. Believe me, the bank will look at the balance sheet and ask you to provide a pro forma balance sheet. But let's face it, most people's eyes will go directly to the P&L and the net income line. At the same time, look at the owner's or officer's compensation line to make sure it's a fair market salary for the job of running the company (especially if it's too high, as that means more profit). Remember the story about the buyer who only looked at the bottom line and didn't think the company made any money (the seller was taking $750,000 in salary).

As a business owner, you know your way around financial statements, so I won't go into detail. The top financial areas to look at include, in alphabetical order, the following:

- Accounts payable
- Accounts receivable
- Accrual versus cash accounting (some firms do accrual on the books and cash basis for taxes or vice versa)
- Assets, anticipated asset replacement (cap ex), and assets excluded from the sale
- Credit policies
- Deposits and deferred revenue (these should be a liability on the balance sheet)
- Inventory
- Work in process and how it's calculated

Ask All the Questions

Two days before closing, a buyer client was shocked to find out the seller paid COD for everything. He had projected thirty-day terms. On my form of nonfinancial questions, it specifically asks about credit policies. When I asked him what the answer to the question about vendor credit was, he hemmed and hawed enough to let me know he never asked the question. Ask questions; it's how you find out about the little things.

During the writing of this book, a banker shared with me how her bank's credit person was "all overanticipated capital expenditures." Obviously, this credit person had some (bad) experience with businesses or deals that didn't pay attention to this. This bank's policy is to grill the buyer and seller on asset replacement, when it's needed, the cost, and factor it into the debt-coverage tests.

Let's discuss a few of the traps or problem areas. First is cash versus accrual accounting and the problems this can cause. (Accrual accounting records income and expenses when booked or incurred, while cash accounting records them when received or paid.) It's a problem when a firm uses one method for financial statements and another for taxes or if they use a hybrid system. Cash accounting offers some real benefits, especially during growth periods. The business can easily adjust revenues and costs at year end to paint an unrealistic picture of the business. Want to pay lower taxes? Delay revenues and accelerate paying bills. Want to show a healthier business? Accelerate revenue collection and delay paying bills.

Besides the hard-to-discover traps of cash accounting, it gets very confusing when one method is used for taxes and another for statements. This is where a CPA earns her keep.

Inventory always leads to some interesting discussions, especially when there's inventory that hasn't sold in a long time (a long time is a relative term and varies by industry). As a buyer, you expect to get useable and salable inventory. Older goods may not be worth tying up your capital or paying interest on. Every so often, I work on a deal where the seller keeps the excess inventory and is free to sell it as best he can, including to the buyer if and when he needs it. One other inventory item applies to manufacturing. Check with your CPA on this, as overhead is supposed to be allocated to inventory not expensed when incurred.

Another area to watch out for is deferred revenue. Customer deposits, prepaid revenues (annual maintenance agreements, for example), and gift cards all need to be recorded as a current liability. They are not recorded as income until the work is done or the gift card redeemed.

Not all businesses do it this way, which is why I mention it. As a buyer, you will expect to get cash to cover the deposits, in addition to normal working capital.

The flip side of deferred revenue is expenses in excess of billings. In other words, the company had done work or made products that haven't been invoiced yet. This should be on the balance sheet as a current asset. The improper recording of these revenue and expense items can distort the income of the company.

Finally, work in process is always an enigma. It's a function of the prior two items, jobs on which the firm is currently working. This is common in construction and manufacturing. It can take some serious work to figure out exactly what's there and what to do with it. On one recent deal, the selling firm was recording *anticipated* deposits before they were received with a debit to accounts receivable and a credit to customer deposits. This created quite a discussion as we figured out how to handle it.

Warning

Sometimes the seller will want to get "paid" for the work in process in addition to the price of the business. They'll say they deserve a share of the profits on those jobs because the sales were made on their watch. The smaller the deal, the greater the chances of this happening. Retiring on the net after tax on a $1 million sale is a lot tougher than retiring on the net after tax of a $5 million sale.

Growth

The tired answer of "We keep the business where it is because we don't want it any larger" translates to "We've tried every way possible to grow, and we're stuck where we are." I've yet to meet a buyer who didn't want to grow the business, and I'm sure you're the same. "Scalable" is a term often used, as is the phrase *take it to the next level.*

As a buyer, I'm sure you want to make sure it can grow after it integrates with your business. Otherwise, why buy it?

As a buyer, you're going to want to know if and how the business can grow. A large part of the answer is the company's marketing program and sales efforts. Doing the right things is the most important part of both marketing and sales because if done regularly and correctly, the results will follow. Concentrate your efforts on what the seller is doing and what she could be doing. If the phone is ringing and sales are made, without much marketing or sales effort, it usually means opportunity.

Delegating

As a sidebar item, here's what I've learned about delegating, other than it's tough for owners to do.

- The owner must be willing to delegate (i.e., give up some responsibility and control). This includes accepting the fact some mistakes will be made during the employee's learning process.
- The employees must be willing and able to accept delegation. This means they must want to advance their careers, or they will decline the added duties.
- There must be a culture of delegation. This usually means the other employees must accept it when the boss delegates and not ostracize the receiving employee because they think he's seeking favor from the boss.

Watch Out for Dependencies

Your diligence must concentrate on what it will be like without the owner while looking at dependencies on a key employee, piece of machinery, or customer.

Talent

As I write this, it's a tough job market—for employers. As much talk as there is about unemployed workers in legacy industries, there are help wanted signs everywhere, for people at all levels. Your investigation in this area needs to concentrate on how the company finds good people, keeps good people, helps them grow, and keeps them happy.

I mentioned before about the employees who felt the buyer was a breath of fresh air. This doesn't mean they were unhappy; they just got happier with the new owner. This is your goal, to find out how you can be a breath of fresh air to the business and its people.

On the flip side, don't be surprised when employees come to you, the new owner, with gripes (we're overworked) or saying they are due for or were promised a raise. Part of your diligence is to review compensation ("When were the last raises given?" is a good question), benefits, reviews, turnover, and other aspects of the employee policies.

Customers

There's more to customer diligence than concentration. Customer concentration is important, and the smaller the business, the greater the chances of a dominant customer or two. When you find this, you have to balance the risk of the customer leaving versus the reward of the customer staying.

But there are other issues to research besides customer diversity or the lack thereof. First is pricing. Are the customers staying because of low prices and willing to tolerate mediocre service because of the price?

Realize not all customers may be paying the same price. An interesting presentation I saw recently discussed categorizing customers by their pricing, margins, and loyalty. In other words, smaller customers paying a higher price are often worth more than larger firms paying a low price (although it does keep the people busy, especially during slow times).

Extremely important is customer satisfaction and loyalty. It's why, on B2B deals, I help my clients by talking to customers. This doesn't mean calling customers and telling them the company is being sold. It means doing a reference check call or a customer satisfaction survey call. If it's a good business, you'll find the customers are happy (and happy to speak with you).

Real-Life Horror Story

The seller convinced the buyer it was too sensitive an industry and therefore too risky to even do a customer satisfaction survey. The attorney told him to kill the deal. I told him to kill the deal until he could talk with the customers. He said he understood the concern and trusted the seller. Too bad for him.

During our due diligence, the number-one customer, 25 percent of annual sales, was doing a "test kitchen" for a new system and invited all the competitors but not their current vendor. They were extremely unhappy with the company and their nickel and diming of them over the years (the product was a major purchase every ten years with upgrades, modifications, service, etc,). By all means, talk with the customers, someway, somehow.

To finish on customers, don't be afraid to research the customer company's health and find out how much customer turnover there is every year.

Customers Can Kill the Deal

I worked on one deal that died because the dominant customer, a public company, was in bad financial health. During discussion of what this meant (to the deal), the customer went bankrupt and closed. I still wonder if and what the seller knew about this.

Here are other categories (in alphabetical order).

Budgeting—ask for current and past budgets and hope they have them. See how close reality matches projections, and realize you need to do your own, if for no other reason than it's a great learning tool.

Competition—you probably know all about the competitors, unless you're expanding into a new geographic area with new competitors. The seller will help you, and these days, the Internet makes tasks like this easier than ever.

Culture—I've covered this a few times, and it's not always easy, but do what you can to determine the firm's culture. Sometimes asking the key employees (before closing) about their suggestions for improvement lets you know if it's an open-to-new-ideas culture or if the owner controls this.

Government regulation—question one on the seller's initial disclosure form asks about this (as do other questions). If you're buying a firm in your industry, you know this. If you're expanding into a new industry or a new city, county, state, or country, this is an area to cover sooner not later.

Human Resources—I live outside of Seattle, one of the most employment regulatory cities in the country. Keeping up on all the rules, regulations, and required filings can be a full-time job. It's why I recommend clients consider an outsourced HR company to make sure they "get it right."

Stories

1) As I'm writing this, two items on this topic came on my radar screen. First, a radio show host was discussing (complaining) about how he missed filing some form for his side business. The city (Seattle) put him through his paces,

made him pay a $275 fee to refile his form, and then made him pay the regular fee and a penalty. By the way, this host is not a conservative, antigovernment person. He's a moderate fed up with this stuff.

2) At about the same time, an article appeared in the *Puget Sound Business Journal* about how Seattle is not friendly to businesses. Here's an example of what's behind this opinion (and why I recommend an HR pro to do it, especially if you're going to a new city).

The owner of a bakery business brought her concerns about the "soaring cost of doing business in Seattle" and how she can keep it alive.

"I'm beholden to six leases. I'm a personal guarantor on those leases," she said. "We could close stores, cut labor, and do all the manufacturing in one space to make up for the costs, but the end result is less jobs."

When she brought her concerns to the Seattle City Council in 2014, explaining that a fifteen-dollar-an-hour minimum wage would increase her bakery's costs by $1 million, one council member told her, "Just raise your prices."

FYI, this councilperson is supposedly an economics teacher by trade. I guess she didn't learn or teach supply, demand, and price elasticity, which are basic tenets of economics 101. Also, if it was so easy to raise prices, why wouldn't the owner have already done it (and made more money all along)?

Industry concentration—it's not only customer concentration that's important, so is industry concentration, especially if it's a cyclical industry. For example, if the auto industry slumps, it's not just Ford, Toyota, or Honda; they'll all be in a slump. If your only customers are in the auto industry, you'll be in a slump, whether you sell products, services, or signage.

Insurance—You know what you have and need (I'm sure). You'd be surprised at the number of times an insurance review saved a lot of money or got better coverage for the same price. Get this done, even if it's after the deal closes. There is a flip side, though. Often you'll find out the seller's company is underinsured, which increases your costs versus historical costs.

Intellectual property—check with your attorney on this, as you need to make sure they have the right copyrights (very easy), trademarks, service marks, patents, and the like. Don't let this come back to haunt you.

Lease—the chances are you'll be getting a new lease, not an assignment of the seller's. In any case, review the lease with a professional and look for "traps." There are many unsophisticated owners who don't pay attention to the lease because "it's never been an issue." Then the buyer gets a lease saying he is responsible for paying for the replacement of the twenty-year-old HVAC system. Also, you won't get a bank loan for a term any longer than the term of the lease, including its options, which means you need a cooperative landlord (there are some exceptions, usually office-based businesses versus manufacturing, retail, or distribution).

Litigation—you'll ask the seller, of course (a question on the seller's initial disclosure asks, "Is there any past, current, pending/anticipated litigation in which the firm is involved?"). The escrow agent or your attorney will do a lien check and background checks, but the sooner you ask, the more time you have to investigate.

Operations—given you're running a business now, your management team and you should have this under control, and I'm sure it's on your list of items to investigate.

Org chart—we all know what it is, but one of the oft-missing items is a place for every job. In other words, if the production manager also does quality control and hiring, there should be a box for each of these positions with her name in each one.

Owners and their duties—this actually should come earlier than the due-diligence process. As stated twice before, what does the owner do on a daily, weekly, and monthly basis? This determines the owner's role, uncovers dependencies, and gives insights. Don't be afraid to probe.

Sales—a good sales team is often worth the price of the company. Do they have a system? Who does sales? How involved is the seller? Can they sell your products to their customers and vice versa? Good salespeople are tough to find (bad ones are easy to find). Get into the weeds on this subject.

Technology—as per the sample of my nonfinancial questions, you want to know how up-to-date the technology is. Are the subscriptions current? Is there any black-market software? You'll also want to know if there are any virus or security issues. A few years before writing this, I helped on a deal where different computers were running Windows 7, XP, 98, and 95. It was quite a mess, and there was definitely a need for hardware upgrades. I also saw a company using DOS for their inventory and then manually transferring the information to QuickBooks (the firm was owned by an accountant). There was a culture shift when the (older) employees had to leave the comfort zone of the old system.

What's Important

I'm on the board of directors of two companies, and at one recent board meeting, the IT person was discussing security and the explosion of ransomware. In fact, there's an acronym that's a play on SaaS (software as a service). He said, "There's now RaaS (ransom as a service), and the Russian mafia is selling it for as little as $175." Read up on this, because if ransomware gets on a system, it quickly encrypts everything, and you have to pay to get it unlocked.

Vendors—vendor concentration is almost as important as customer concentration with some banks (so it should be with you). Bankers have told me how they've held up loans as they investigated the vendor (especially when there's vendor concentration), just to make sure the primary supplier was in good condition. Also, be concerned with credit polices (see a previous story on this).

Overconfidence Makes for a Self-Inflicted Wound

All of my chapter-ending stories are good news. But all examples can't be great, can they? Here's an example of doing it wrong, and it shows how sloppy due diligence plus overconfidence can lead to disaster.

Two people referred me to the fairly new owner of a printing business, actually two printing businesses. His intentions were correct; he wanted a larger company, overhead spread over a larger base, more customers, more and better equipment, and so on.

Here's where it went wrong: he overpaid, at least for the second one. I've worked on enough deals—and analyzed many more companies—to quickly recognize this. His second deal was predicated on the following:

- His overconfidence of what he could do and the speed in which he could do it (good diligence would have brought him down to earth and reduced his buyer fever).
- A smooth and complete integration of the two companies, with slightly different customer bases and equipment.
- Growth, which didn't occur at all, much less as projected. (This is the big one; if your deal and payments are based on growth, you're in trouble.)

Your deal has to make sense, without everything having to fall into place in an efficient manner. There appeared to be nothing wrong with either of these printing companies. What was wrong were the deals and the deals' dependence on the sum being greater than the parts (added together).

Having had clients who never ran out of questions (my Columbo client) and clients whom I had push to ask more questions, I can tell you there's a middle ground, which is the leap of faith. Also, there are a few final points.

- One thing to notice is a lot of the chapter-end stories emphasize paying attention to the details before, during, and after the transaction. The big stuff is obvious. It's the finer points you need to pay attention to.
- It's a tedious process, and only you (meaning your team and you personally) can do (most of) it, as it's your deal.
- As Bob says in the final section of this chapter, don't make assumptions.
- The seller will get overwhelmed and wonder why there are so many questions. This will lead to deal fatigue.
- Most of the diligence is not the numbers.
- Don't forget the vehicles and equipment. Don't just look at them; inspect them, and see maintenance logs.
- No matter what, you have to meet key employees and talk to the vendors and customers (B2B businesses) before closing.

Why They Made an Acquisition

Bob Brencic is the owner of Trestle Property Services LLC (www.trestlecm.com). Trestle provides management services to associations, primarily condo associations. When he made his first acquisition in 2014, Bob knew this was a very fragmented industry with a lot of small lifestyle businesses.

After a successful corporate career, he was "ready to do my own thing" and not work corporate anymore. He didn't want a franchise and knew buying was faster and would get him infrastructure. From the start, he researched and targeted the property management industry.

His first acquisition was small but gave him the platform and experience. He then bought a much larger firm, about one year after the first one. Here are some things he learned from buying a larger firm.

1. He should have done more customer due diligence. He made some assumptions in this area he should not have made. Because of this, he lost customers, some because a manager left after the sale and some because they weren't happy with the seller (the seller was eighty years old, and the business practices had slipped over his last couple of years).
2. If an employee had a noncompete agreement but it can't be found, shut the deal down until it's resolved (he got burned).
3. Pay attention to the culture (the best you can).
4. Ask all the due-diligence questions; don't just check off the boxes (because you're in the industry).
5. Realize it's not for the faint of heart, and don't expect too much too fast.

These are some great warnings, and if Bob could go back in time, he'd do things a little differently. That said, here are his final comments during our interview: "I'm really happy! It turned out well."

CHAPTER 10

GLENGARRY GLEN ROSS* (GOING FOR THE CLOSE)

Much of this chapter is the same as in my book *Buying a Business that Makes You Rich* because getting the deal done is same as it was when I wrote that book.

On the Road to Closing

Earlier, I provided an outline of my process from information gathering through due diligence. Here's a more detailed outline, from letter of intent to closing.

- Signed letter of intent
- Due diligence—legal, accounting, nonfinancial factors, and other relevant items
- The bank's commitment letter
- Waiver of all due-diligence items except talking to customers, employees, vendors, and funding
- Signed purchase and sale agreement with contingencies for the items in the preceding

---

* The title of this chapter is the title of a 1992 film on real-estate sales, "predatory closers," and closing the sale, although everything we do is on the up and up. So it's time to close the sale (no buyer or seller remorse here).

- Completion of final due diligence with customers, employees, and vendors
- Bank's final approval
- At closing, signed bank documents and updated, contingency-free purchase and sale forms

There are many, many moving parts to a closing. A good escrow attorney will get most of them, but there are some you or your staff have to do.

The following is from a document I give my clients when we start working together, even though much of it doesn't need to be done until two months prior to closing. This list was compiled by getting input from eight to ten clients who had closed on deals in the two years prior to when I wrote this. A lot of these items are the nagging little administrivia things that drive many people nuts, but they must be done.

What to Do When Buying a Business

Government
If a new entity is being formed for this transaction, complete these items.

- Determine legal structure.
- Do federal and state registrations.
- Check county and city regulations.
- Pick your name and register it (register the seller's name and any dbas if you're not doing a new entity).
- Obtain state and local business licenses.
- Register with the State Department of Revenue.
- Obtain an employer identification number.
- Complete all tax forms; this includes registering for worker compensation insurance (whether government or private), sales tax, unemployment insurance, personal property taxes, and any other requirements.
- Get necessary local permits and licenses.

- If you will have a registered agent other than yourself, get it registered with your state.
- Do S corporation election and filing.

In all cases, complete the following tasks:

- Get any hazardous material and environmental reports, if applicable.
- Confirm seller's existing corporation or LLC existence.
- If asset purchase, dissolve seller's entity or have him relinquish the trade name to you.

Nongovernment

Here's a checklist of most of the nongovernment tasks you'll need to accomplish.

- Bank—deposits, credit card processing, lines of credit, and so on
- Utilities—long distance, local, cellular, and the like changed over.
- Internet, website, shippers (FedEx, UPS).
- Copyrights, trademarks, and other intellectual property, including trade name registration.
- Insurance—property, liability, vehicle, life (bank may require), health, disability, and so on
- New business cards.
- New lease secured or a lease assignment.
- Software licenses, passwords, and so on
- Off-balance-sheet items like equipment leases, advertising contracts, and accrued time off
- Employment agreements/noncompete agreements, W-9s, and W-4s.
- Contracts with vendors, customers, and others.
- Customer lists including *all* contact information.
- Signage, printing, labels, and so on
- Vehicle registrations transferred.

Financial

Your accountant will have a longer list I'm sure and start with this.

- Books and records (What system? Who does it? Does your CPA approve of it?).
- Vendor list (Must you apply for credit?).
- Closing reports, liens, taxes due, and so forth
- Prorated expenses and revenues, including accounting for customer deposits for future work and the cash needed to fulfill such work.
- Postclosing settlement date (to cover late billings, invoices, proratas, etc.).

Life insurance is a timely issue. Your bank usually will (and the seller may) require it. It takes six to eight weeks to get a policy issued, so you must start early.

Disclaimer

The above is not a due-diligence form or checklist. It supplements your due-diligence forms. It is designed as a guide for the little things it takes to prepare for closing; get your entity off the ground and ensure a smooth transition. It is not guaranteed to be all-inclusive (as all deals and situations are different). Items are not listed in any order. If you are unsure about the sequence of events, just call me. If you find anything missing, please let me know so I can add it to the list.

Time Line

Following is a sample closing time line, with sample dates. Start filling in the tasks and dates once you have agreed to an offer (at least verbally). Each deal is different, and this form is not meant to be all encompassing. It may represent tasks not required for your deal. Check off each item when it's completed. It's easy to create in Word, or you can e-mail me for a copy of this template (john@johnmartinka.com).

Done	Action	Target Date
———	Preliminary Committal Letter from Bank	
———	LOI signed	
———	All financial information for bank, from seller	
———	Buyer applies for life insurance	
———	Package to bank(s)	
———	Buyer-seller initial due diligence meeting	
———	Bank package to credit department	
———	Due diligence – next milestone	
———	Legal documents – drafting started	
———	Meet landlord – discuss lease	
———	Bank review completed	
———	Financial due diligence approved	
———	Buyer calls customers as "references" or similar	
———	Bank request for tax returns (form 4506, seller signs)	
———	Bank orders business valuation and home appraisal	
———	Landlord wavier draft-language (from bank)	
———	Escrow agent alerted	
———	Asset allocation from CPAs	
———	Final draft of legal documents	
———	Promissory note	
———	Security agreement to band	
———	Lease – tentative approval by both parties	
———	Life insurance approved	
———	Business valuation completed	
———	Home appraisal completed	
———	Bank documents ready	
———	All docs ready for signing	
———	Buyer meets employees	
———	Signing of subordination agreement by Seller	
———	Buyer's money in Escrow Account	

While this example is from a real deal, we know all deals and time lines are different. The point of the written time line is to organize the project and provide the lead times all parties will need to understand. I like to work backward. Determine an estimated closing date, and then ask the bank, lawyers, and others what kind of lead time they need to meet that date. We then put their dates in the time line to make it feasible (with a cushion in all areas).

The Bank and Your Closing

Notice that about two-thirds of the tasks in the time line involve the bank. If you're not going to use a bank for your deal, many, but not all, of these tasks will be reduced or disappear. For now, let's assume there is a bank involved.

The bank controls the process, the time line, and the closing date; there's no way around it. Note that the time line starts after you have a term sheet from at least one bank and at least a verbal agreement on price, terms, and conditions (or an LOI). Then your efforts are concentrated on the following areas:

- Getting the bank everything they need to give final and formal approval.
- Having the lawyers draft and finalize the purchase and sale agreement (PSA).*
- Getting all the administrivia mentioned in the closing checklist handled, including a lease or lease assignment, vendors, employment agreements, and more.
- Completing due diligence, including talking to the customers and key employees.

*I recommend that you have your attorney draft the PSA and related documents. It will cost you more, but you will usually get a document with "warranties and representations" that will be fairer to both sides. If there's a note or a lease from the seller, it is the obligation of the seller and her attorney to provide you with the note and lease.

Your Team's Involvement

This is where your team gets active. Obviously, your attorney takes the lead and the most active role. Make sure your attorney (and hopefully the seller's attorney) likes to draft and edit documents with the intent that the other side will find them fair. It's too easy, and I've seen too many instances, where one attorney wants 95 percent of the risk on the other side. This does nothing but increase legal bills, cause frustration on both sides, and delay the deal. Busy attorneys (who are also good) will avoid this, as they have many clients, and just want to get the deal done. By all means, don't use a litigator and hope the seller doesn't use one. They love to negotiate.

Make Sure the Attorneys Play Well Together

There are three primary criteria when it comes to attorneys for the deal:

- Both parties need attorneys experienced in buy-sell deals.
- They must be used to working in the size range of your deal (not a lot smaller or larger).
- They must be able to share the sandbox (i.e., play well together).

The last point means don't you get and hope the seller doesn't get a brother-in-law who's a divorce attorney, a litigator (they'll argue—not just negotiate—everything they can), or a real-estate attorney.

In one recent case, the seller's attorney was obviously not familiar with buy-sell deals and bank financing. He inserted language (and strongly advised his clients) about not agreeing to standard bank language and policies. Of course, it created some conflict with the seller (until his other advisors clued him in to the real world).

Your CPA will need to work with the seller's CPA to determine the asset allocation. This is where they both earn their keep. You want as many write-offs as possible, and the seller wants as low a tax bill as he or she can get. My experience is that the emphasis will be on depreciable assets, the noncompete agreement, and the training allocation—the rest being current assets and goodwill. How retained debt fits into this is for your CPA to determine.

Your CPA may also help you with financial due diligence; spot-checking audits; and analyzing the accounting system, chart of accounts, and other tactical accounting-related matters. There is no set agenda here; part of it depends on your knowledge of accounting matters and your willingness to do some of this work. I've had clients bring in their CPA for a few days to do it all, and I've had others go in themselves to do mini-audits (e.g., compare bank statements to deposit books to the accounting entries and financial statements for particular months, do the same for expense tracking, or analyze the sales pipeline).

As mentioned, other members of your team now may get involved. I've had clients whose team comprised their banker, lawyer, CPA, and me and others who used some of the following:

- A CFO to help with cash-flow projections, budgets, and so on
- Human resource experts when there were employee issues that could be a problem.
- Environmental consulting firms to do studies of the property.
- Equipment experts to analyze the useful life of the machinery.
- Commercial real-estate agents to help with determining the fair market rent and to help with the lease.

Real-Life Story: Don't Skimp on Advice; You Get What You Pay For

Here's how not to use your team. My client was in the process of closing on a deal to buy a similar business close to his geographic area. At the same time, he was looking at another acquisition in a different state (for which he didn't hire me).

The attorney I recommended helped him with his Washington deal but wasn't licensed in the other state. He tried to help, but the out-of-state attorney came across as inexperienced in transactions and wouldn't even talk to the Washington attorney.

I later met with this owner and determined he didn't hire a CPA for the second transaction. And his attorney truly didn't know deals. A big part of this deal was an earn out (percentage of sales over a number of years). It was structured to be goodwill, meaning a fifteen-year amortization. It should have been a royalty or similar to give the buyer an immediate write-off.

The bottom line was with the payments to the seller, taxes on the profit, and amortization of the goodwill, he had extremely low cash flow from this deal. This will continue until his earn-out payments are completed, at which time he'll have accelerated cash flow because of the amortization write-off and no payments to the seller. However, most companies need the cash flow now, if for no other reason than to be emotionally happy with the deal.

Purchase and Sale Agreement

This is the heart of all deals. By the time you arrive at this point, there should be very little negotiating left to do. This doesn't mean negotiations are over; the attorneys will have lengthy discussions about warranties and representations. In simple layman terms, these are the clauses where both buyer and seller state that everything they have presented about the business and themselves is true and correct. Attorney friends tell me this is the topic they spend most of their time on, once the first draft is completed.

Most attorneys look for a fair divide within the reps and warranties clauses. Occasionally, you'll see an attorney who wants full protection for his client and almost none for the other side. When it happens, it's a pain, but it doesn't happen that often. This is why I ask attorneys to draft contracts that they would find fair if they were on the receiving end of the said contract.

From a nonlegal perspective, here are the most important items you should be concerned with:

Warranties and Representations

As just mentioned, the warranties and representations section are key. This is where both attorneys earn their fees. You want the seller to represent what she has told you is true and correct. You also want to have some recourse if you find something that was materially misrepresented. Work closely with your attorney on this, especially on the indemnification section.

Real-Life Story: Can't Hide Everything

The buyer had acquired a computer business that built machines, did repairs, and sold parts. While the business had a storefront, the majority of the sales were to businesses and government.

About six months after closing, the owner looked at the morning paper, and the headline said his business was under investigation for selling black-market Microsoft software. It seems the seller had received two "cease and desist" letters from Microsoft, and not only did he ignore them for the most part, he also didn't disclose this to his broker, his attorney, or the buyer—even though he was directly asked the question, in writing, about potential litigation.

Because there was a strong purchase and sale agreement, a good attorney, and a seller note (which gave him leverage over the seller), the buyer survived this. In fact, a few months later, the buyer said that the headlines were a boon to his business. People remembered the company name and forgot how and why they heard about the business.

Noncompete Agreement

Sometimes it's a separate document and sometimes a section in the contract. It's also very important, especially if the seller is not at or beyond the typical retirement age. I've seen buyers want very tight conditions and others who don't care too much about it.

Work with your attorney so it's realistic and enforceable. Realize you can have a lot stronger noncompete with the seller than with the employees. The seller is trading the value of the business in return for not competing with you (and for the money). If the seller wants a very loose or short noncompete, you should wonder why.

Asset Allocation

We've discussed asset allocation a few times previously, and this is where it gets memorialized. Your CPA and the seller's CPA will work to find common ground. As stated, the biggest issue for the seller will be any possible taxation at ordinary income rates versus capital gains rates. The common culprits here are depreciation recapture, the value of the non-compete, and the value of training (of you by the seller).

You will usually want to accelerate depreciation of the assets in lieu of the fifteen-year write-off for goodwill. Be sure to pay attention to all taxes. For example, in Washington, the fixed assets are subject to sales tax (at over 9 percent) if they are assets not used to manufacture a product. While in the long run it's better to pay the sales tax and redepreciate, in the short run, it can be a large hit to initial cash flow.

Closing

As mentioned, often the signing of the agreement is not done at closing. One huge reason for an advanced signing is that the seller wants the buyer to be fully committed before interviewing the customers and employees. The agreement will have contingencies for these interviews and perhaps other items, which often includes the funding of the approved loan.

On the flip side, it is not uncommon to have the closing after the effective date, meaning the documents are backdated. This happens if it's close to the year, quarter, or month end and it's just simpler to backdate than to prorate expenses like rent, payroll, and similar, plus have double tax reporting for a short period.

Whether you sign in advance, on the date of closing, or after (backdate), expect that all the details won't be worked out at that time. You will most likely have a settlement date between 60 and 120 days after closing. Some of your down payment may stay in escrow to cover any payables not recorded as of closing, uncollectable receivables, or other costs that materialized.

Here are a few things that your attorney, the escrow agent, or you will want to handle (in addition to what has already been mentioned).

- The titles for any registered assets (often vehicles).
- Confirmation of the amount and value of inventory.
- Verification and inspection of all assets.
- All notifications to government and nongovernment organizations.
- Intellectual property filings.
- All computer-related licenses, warranties, passwords, and so forth
- Off-balance-sheet items (leases) and renewals of items like advertising.

Realize that if you have an asset sale structure, the seller will retain her legal entity, bank accounts, tax ID number, and similar. The seller will have to file all necessary tax forms and handle her portion of employee benefits, pension deposits, and the like.

The All-Important Transition Plan

The transition technically starts the day after closing. Realistically, it starts once you've both signed an LOI. Your due diligence does double duty. It's both confirmation of what you've initially been told, your first glimpse into cultural, operational insights, and the start of your initial training.

As with anything in business, having a structured transition plan accelerates your success. Let's look at a sample transition plan. This plan is for a company that is a sales and service organization, so you'll have to adjust it if your business is in a different industry, and you'll need to tweak it even if you're buying a sales and service company. Realize that you may want the seller out long before the official transition period ends. One client told his seller that the seller would be on-call by phone after only one week of personal training (the seller didn't mind at all).

Ask the seller what are the five most important things you need to know and accomplish sooner versus later. Write these down. Then do it for the next five and so on. This is a great starting place. The list will include much of the following:

- Sales—products, customers, industry and competition, value proposition, and key selling tactics.
- Finance—systems, procedures, reports, inventory management, and who does what.
- Human resources—management team, key employees, culture, procedures, policy manual, and who does HR (the owner shouldn't).
- Operations—varies by industry, but don't forget to train the buyer on customer service.
- Growth—the plan, its tactics, competitive advantage, what's worked, what hasn't worked, and why.

Some initial transition tactics that have worked well include the following:

- The buyer hosts an introductory lunch, gets to meet the employees, discusses his plans, and, most important, lets the employees know he's not making any changes—especially with staff so they realize their jobs are secure.
- The seller implements a day-by-day schedule with a little bit of everything for the buyer.
- The buyer shadows the seller the first week or so, just to see what he does and have the opportunity to ask questions and observe operations.
- The seller plans a one-week vacation, three to four weeks into the transition. This lets the employees know things are OK without the seller there, and so they definitely know who the new boss is.

The following is a sample transition and training plan that a (very detailed) buyer put together. It's overly ambitious and probably wasn't adhered to because there's still a business to run, but it outlines very well how this subject should be approached. The seller wants to get out in whatever time the agreement specifies, so the more organized you are, the better off you'll both be.

Strategic Transition and Training Plan

This is a sample only. Your plan may look nothing like this.
This was for a sales, installation, and service company.

Before Close

- Continue building the business plan.
- Continue to gather information and learn the industry.
- Ensure corporate affairs are in order.
- Establish financial and banking account relationships (all the things on the closing checklist).

First Thirty Days

- Review any operating plans, performance, and personnel data.
- Meet with employees one on one, and ask how they see the business improving.
- Assess how things are going and where you can add value.
- What are the challenges and opportunities?
- Do you still need the seller around?

Thirty to Sixty Days

Discuss preliminary findings with the seller (after thirty days).

What are the key issues?

- Culture
- Sales effort

- Restructuring duties
- Team capabilities (Are changes needed?)
- Customer relationships
- Vendor relationships
- Other
- Do you still need the seller around?

Sixty to Ninety Days

- By this time, you should have a good understanding of the business.
- Where should you focus your efforts? Sales, operations, growth, or culture?
- What is the seller's role in the future (consult, disappear)?

Training Plan—Tactical

The following table outlines a tactical training schedule of items to consider on a weekly basis. (This is for the first week only, which is why I said this plan is overly ambitious.) Provide this to the seller, get her input, and move on it.

Week 1

Sales

- Review basic sales strategy (leads, follow-up, bids, etc.).
- Spend time with the salespeople as they call on customers. How are leads generated? What is their style and approach?
- Get up to speed on all products.
- Schedule introductions to suppliers and vendor training.

- Visit a few local customers (don't plan the major sales training this week).
- Plan major sales calls for next week.

Operations

- Listen to and begin answering phone calls.
- Figure out the scheduling system.
- Determine how jobs are bid and how the software is used.
- Visit a job in progress.
- Schedule time to spend with each technician.
- Spend time with key people if available.
- Determine what type of network is set up, if any, and reconfigure if necessary.

Accounting

- Establish a new company in the accounting system.
- Sit with the bookkeeper to learn exactly what she does.
- Download all information on company policies.
- Set up outside payroll services.
- Apply for fleet fuel cards and company credit cards.
- Visit CPA to finalize company setup.
- Ensure online bank account software and hardware for remote deposits is set up and working.

HR

- Review all employee records.
- Download all system documentation.
- Gather remaining signatures needed for corporate docs.

- Finalize team member assessments and their capabilities.
- Ensure all licensing with state L&I/employment security is transferred.

Goals

By the end of week one, you will have the following:

- A general understanding of how the sales process works in this business
- Observed live sales calls
- Ensured everyone is enrolled in new benefit plans as applicable
- A general understanding of all products and services the business offers
- The new accounting system up and running
- Established payroll procedures
- Been introduced either by phone or in person to key stakeholders or have meetings scheduled
- Installed remote access systems to allow you to access the system from home

The seller's job is to help you achieve so much success that you can pay off your note ahead of schedule. During the deal phase, it may have seemed you were adversaries. Now you're teammates with common goals—to get her out of there, have the business thrive, and have everyone be wildly happy.

Final Thoughts

As we wrap up, let's make sure everything is put in perspective. While growth by acquisition makes dollars and sense, it isn't for everybody; the proverbial stars must align. There's a lot to do, but it can get you a jump-start on growth and a larger platform for organic growth. As you've noticed, while I believe in the strategy, it has to fit your overall plan.

While I didn't start out with the idea of interviewing owners about their growth by acquisition experience, I came to realize those interviews contain a lot of great nuggets of information. Pay attention to what these people say, and learn from their lessons (as well as from the rest of the book).

Why They Made an Acquisition

For the final chapter, let's do two!

Bobby Holt and Lee Falck own Pacific Tool Inc. in Redmond, Washington, (www.pacifictool.com) as well as two coffee-roasting companies they bought and combined. Bobby and Lee have a history of acquisitions, having bought their first company in the early twenty-first century and sold it to a public company a number of years later. At the time of this writing, we are looking for other opportunities.

Bobby told me acquisitions let them grow faster and into markets sooner, in months not years. Growth is a primary motivator, as they find it time-consuming and sometimes painful to get to the end result. This is because he recognizes it's a very inefficient market; plus, you (the buyer) have to manage the seller, the process, and valuation expectations.

His tips are to realize it takes time and is a distraction from day-to-day operations. Also, the integration is work. He knows the seller will also spend a lot of time during the transaction.

Their coffee company integrations were easy. Pacific Tool needed to be more gradual; they changed the culture as they learned how to understand the customers and the employees and let them know what success means. One key is to be transparent.

Mark Lotzkar is the CEO of Pacific Metals in Vancouver, BC, Canada (www.pacificmetals.ca) (they have a sister company, Regional Recycling), a company started in 1900 and now with its third generation of owners and fourth generation of family members in the business.

Since 1990, they have made ten acquisitions. Mark's comment about why they make acquisitions is "growth means security." In their industry, it's vitally important they integrate themselves into the supply chain, as their biggest risk is losing access to scrap.

While he finds the process to be a bit of necessary drudgery, he loves it when the deal closes, and he gets to meet the new team and assure them their future is secure with his firm. Then it's on to the next one.

His advice is to be patient (these things take time), be doggedly perseverant to go after it, and believe in yourself and your team, as it's not just one person who gets it done (on both sides).

APPENDICES

APPENDIX A

Putting Together a Business-Loan Package

From Lisa Forrest, SBA Lending Professional with Live Oak Bank, 425-999-2042

The following is written as a primer for sellers, but buyers can use it to make sure their target company will make the banker's job as easy as possible, with a quicker approval.

How the seller prepares his or her business for sale and how the buyer applies for a loan can help increase your odds for a successful sale with more cash to you!

Business owners can improve their exit and sale process by considering the perspective of their buyer. If acquisition financing will be the source of funding, sellers can increase the probability of a lender approving a loan for their buyer through thoughtful preparation and attention to details. The US Small Business Administration (SBA) loan program is an excellent avenue that banks can use for business-acquisition financing. The SBA has certain guidelines and parameters that every participating bank must follow when offering this type of loan; however, each lender will have his own requirements and terms, at times causing increased confusion and some amount of trepidation. While the sale process can be unsettling for business owners, there are definite steps that can be followed to increase control over critical aspects of the sales process when it comes to their buyer's acquisition financing.

Here are nine points for the seller to consider that can help make his business a stronger candidate for SBA acquisition financing:

1. Business owner planning and preparation—planning to sell your business can take years. Knowing when it is the right time to sell takes thought and preparation. For most of the successful acquisitions I have been involved with, preparation started months, and in most cases, several years prior to the actual loan/acquisition close. Being a prepared and organized seller is key.

2. Exit strategy advisors—because your business is usually one of your biggest investments, having outside advice is generally going to increase your opportunities for success. As owners, you are experts in your industry and have built a successful business; however, when it comes to selling your gem that you have spent years creating, I have observed that outside expertise and perspective will usually serve the seller well. See #1 above.

3. Buyers and lenders will have similar perspectives. The buyer and their lender will have the same questions and want to see the same documentation, books, and records. The buyer's and the banker's interests are well aligned, so when you think about questions that the bank will have, they are most often the same questions that your buyer will have. This is an important notion to understand because a seller should be preparing for the buyer and the banker in much the same way.

4. Buyer "due-diligence team"—as a banker specializing in business-acquisition financing for more than twenty years, I have come to appreciate the buyer who has his due-diligence team. And, as a seller, you should also come to appreciate this as well. When the buyer comes with outside advisors, it signals to me that he is serious and prepared to take the process all the way through to a close. This team usually consists of a CPA, attorney, banker, and buyer representative. And for sellers who are prepared, having

a buyer with a team of trusted, experienced acquisition advisors will actually help move the process along faster.

5. Documentation for a bank loan package—having your financial documents organized, up to date, and ready for the buyer's lender are critical. Generally, the lender will *initially* require three years of business tax returns, year-end financial statements, year-to-date financial statements, including profit and loss statement, balance sheet, accounts receivable and payables aging statements, and debt schedule. The lender will also require three years' personal-tax returns on the buyer, personal financial statement, and complete résumé. The buyer's background, industry experiences, or complementary work history are also critical for consideration. Letter of intent on the transaction will be required for initial underwriting. If available, copies of leases are helpful at the outset. These are the basic documentation requirements to get the package started, and additional information will be required along the way, depending on each specific project.

6. Lender underwriting...business considerations—once your buyer has submitted a complete loan package, the bank's underwriter will generally take about two to three weeks to thoroughly review the loan request. Each lender will have his own credit policies, but because the business-acquisition project is usually always lacking full collateralization, lenders will generally all require acceptable debt service. Your business's existing cash flow must show the ability to cover the requested bank debt and appropriate salary for buyer's personal-living needs, plus a "cushion" or margin for error on top. The lender will also analyze performance trends. An organized seller will have prepared, in advance, explanations for any unusual adjustments, seller discretionary add-backs, or negative performance issues. Having written statements at the ready for the buyer's lender always impresses. Having access to the seller's CPA can also be a help to the lender during underwriting, especially if there are interesting adjustments or complicated add-backs to more clearly understand.

7. Lender underwriting and buyer qualifications—the lender is going to look for the following in your buyer: industry and/or complementary work expertise, resources available for down payment and postclosing personal liquidity, collateral support, credit score, and secondary sources of repayment. A transition plan from the buyer will also be critical to underwriting. Is there a well-thought-out and written plan to transition the seller out and the buyer in? The collaboration and planning between seller and buyer in this regard is often overlooked during initial LOI conversations, and this is one of the most important aspects to a successful seller exit.

8. Mitigations—in a perfect world, the lender would review a project with 100 percent positive trends in all areas of debt service, performance trends, buyer industry experience, and liquidity. In all my years of SBA lending, it has been a rare occurrence to have a project with perfect scores in all areas. There is a real art to helping put an SBA acquisition project together. As lenders, we are always trying to find the right blend of loan amount, buyer down payment, and seller carry-back financing to balance the particular strengths and challenges of each specific acquisition project. The more prepared the seller is for the buyer's underwriting process, the more he can play a positive role in providing critical information and being sensitive to what the buyer will be going through on his or her end.

9. Be open to the financing process. I don't mean to sound too dramatic, but lenders are going to get nosy. And please understand that the lender asks all these questions and requires the documentation simply to educate himself on the merit of your specific project. I never seek to offend but only to understand. I have the utmost respect for business owners who have spent years building something of value, and my goal is to reach a win-win-win for the seller, buyer, and bank.

Appendix B

From multiple banks (some requirements are mandatory, and others vary by bank and deal)

Loan Request

- SBA application to be completed for applicant (*proposed borrower*)
- Business/transition plan (*a narrative on buyer's complementary skill set—what is the plan on replacing seller, employees who are transitioning, and so on*), including two-year projections of profit and loss to include detailed assumptions for projected revenues and expenses
- Copy of executed letter of intent and, when ready, executed purchase agreement, including asset allocation
- Transmittal document (form attached—set of questions that will allow our UW team to get a better understanding of the deal). Please answer questions that apply to your specific loan request. If answers can be found in other documents, such as business valuation questionnaire, transition plan, broker

offering memorandum, and so on, please copy and paste onto transmittal).

- Lease agreement
- Source of equity injection and supporting documentation
- Copy of seller carry-back loan (if any) with portion considered equity to be on full standby (no principal or interest), two years minimum
- Business valuation (third-party valuation to be ordered by the bank)
- Entity documentation

Borrower (if an existing business entity)

- Interim financial statement (balance sheet, profit and loss, A/R and A/P aging, debt schedule)—current within sixty days of application
- Last three years of federal business tax returns (to include all schedules, forms, K1s, and statements)
- If most recent tax return is not available, please provide a copy of extension with proof of payment for any taxes due
- Three years of year-end financial statements (balance sheet and profit and loss)

Personal Guarantors (must be provided by individuals with 20 percent or more ownership)

- Management résumé
- Authorization release information
- Disclosures and application signature
- SBA Form 413—Personal Financial Statement (*spouse signature required*)

- SBA Form 1919—*This must be completed by each officer and director of the borrowing entity, regardless of ownership interest*
- SBA Form 912—Statement of Personal History (*only required if you answered yes to questions 1–3 on SBA 1919*); *additional documentation/processing will be required for any yes answers*
- Last three years' complete copy of federal personal-tax returns (to include all schedules, forms, K1s, and statements)
- If most recent year tax return is not available, please provide a copy of extension with proof of payment for any taxes due
- K1s for *all* affiliates as listed on Schedule E of personal-tax returns
- Three years of W2s if applicable
- Copy of legal permanent resident alien card (front and back) with executed INS-USCIS borrower authorization form (*only applies to non-US citizens*)

Insurance

- All collateral must be insured for replacement value
- General liability insurance
- Flood insurance on all assets in a flood zone
- Life insurance in the amount of the loan

Business Being Acquired/Operating Company

- Business history (SBA application pages 4 and 5)
- Interim financial statement (balance sheet, profit and loss, A/R and A/P aging, debt schedule—required if debt is to be assumed with purchase transaction)—current within sixty days of application
- Inventory listing dated the same date as the interim statements
- Trailing twelve-month financial statement, on a month-to-month basis

- Work-in-progress report for each three fiscal year-ends and YTD, if applicable
- Equipment listing (serial numbers should be provided for any item with an estimated value exceeding $5,000)
- Bank to do a complete walk-through to verify equipment
- Last three years' complete copy of federal business tax returns (to include all schedules, forms, K1s, and statements)
- If most recent tax return is not available, please provide a copy of extension with proof of payment for any taxes due
- Three years of year-end financial statements (balance sheet and profit and loss)

Same company information for any affiliate owner companies (any businesses/affiliates associated with borrowing entity/guarantor where there is 20 percent or more ownership or controlling interest)

Additional Information—SBA Requirement

- Form 159 is to be filled out whenever an agent (other than a lender service provider) is paid by either a small business applicant or a lender. It is signed by the applicant and the lender.
  a. If the borrower paid a packaging fee upfront to a third party, please have him provide us a completed 159 at the time of application as indicated by the samples. We can fill in the loan # later.
  b. If fees paid are over $2,500, applicant must itemize.

If applicable, the following items will be required during the processing stage or unless deemed necessary by credit during the underwriting stage:

- Business valuation questionnaire
- Franchise agreements/dealership agreements (*if applicable*)
- Letter of explanation for *any* bankruptcies, judgments, lawsuits, liens, foreclosure, and so on (*if applicable*)

- SBA IRS Form 4506-T for applicant/operating company, business being acquired, all business and individual guarantors as applicable—must be *signed and dated* (*electronic signatures are not acceptable*)
- Contact information sheet
- Title report if available (*real-estate transactions only*)
- Construction/tenant improvement documents as available—*refer to SBA application checklist* (*if applicable*)
- Environmental questionnaire (*real-estate transactions only*)
- Property description/access contact (real-estate transactions only) needed to engage third party
- Borrower org chart (if more than one borrower)

Appendix C

Master Due-Diligence List

U se this list judicially. If you aren't buying the company as a whole (a stock sale), you may not need many of the legal documents (check with your attorney). Trying to get all of this information will overwhelm any seller. The questions are important and are bigger-picture questions than those on some of the other forms.

Establish Responsibilities and Time Line

Legal Documents

Is the corporation (or LLC) in good standing?
Articles of incorporation
Foreign jurisdictions
Officers/directors owners
Subsidiaries and/or affiliates
Special shareholder rights (i.e., preemptive rights or other agreements)
Minutes of board meetings (three years)
By-laws

What capital has been invested or loaned to business?
How has company been capitalized until now?

Company's Business

Describe the nature of the business.
Describe each line of products and services sold.
Describe proposed emphasis and direction of business.
Is there an intention to widen the range of products and services sold?
Are there any limitations to products, tariffs, licenses, copyrights, and the like?
Intellectual property¾trademarks, trade names, copyrights, patents, software, trade secrets, other
The method of sales, contracts with suppliers
Contracts with other companies
Are subcontractors used and for what?
Are there any long-term contracts with subcontractors or others?
A list of competitors and a description of their products
What do you know about the competitors' financing and technical resources?
What is the ease or difficulty to enter this business? *In detail*
Copies of technical information, trademarks, trade names, copyrights, and licenses
Copies of any major contracts
Description of distribution channels

Industry Growth

What is the estimated growth rate of the industry in the next five years?
What factors will affect growth in the future?
Are prices, industry-wide, stable or increasing?

Marketing Strategy

What are the marketing objectives?
How will the objectives be implemented?
What marketing effort is required?
What expense is projected?

Marketing Plan

How many people are involved in marketing? Who are they?
What are historical sales increases/decreases by line (percentages)?
What are the sales projections by product and percentage of future revenue?

Product Pricing

How are products and services priced?
Will there be any price changes in the future?
How does pricing compare with competitive and comparable products?
Review actual invoices with major customers (to check for discounts, special deals, etc.).

Customer Analysis

Who are the customers?
What are the trends in this customer group?
Customer list by volume of sales (three years)
What is the procedure to sell products and services?
Copies of all client agreements or contracts
What will be the determining factors to a buying decision?
Are sales controlled by a few high-priced, well-connected salespeople?

Facilities Required

What facilities changes will be required in the future—size, description?
Technology requirements, hardware, software, licensing agreements, and the like

Employees

List of officers and directors (and key employees)
Résumés of officers and directors (and key employees)
List of all employees, salary, date of hire, and title
Copies of employment agreements
Employee turnover—out of the ordinary?
Compensation schedule for owners, officers, and key employees (including bonus plan)

Due-Diligence List

List of shareholders and percentage ownership
Company's attorney, CPA, insurance broker, health-insurance broker, and so on
Company's bank and statements, deposit books, check register, QuickBooks file, and so on
Environmental reports
Employee manuals
Copies of company leases
List of all major assets¾current, at fair market value
Brochures and other marketing materials
Financial statements last five years
Financial statements, monthly for one to two years
Accounts receivable aging report
List of all debts and liabilities

Copies of the last five years' federal income-tax returns (4506 with IRS if needed)

Copies of three to five years' state sales and use tax returns

Copies of all agreements, loan agreements, notes, pledge agreements, and security

Copies of all profit sharing or deferred compensation plans

Business plan

Litigation history and anticipated (both ways), court search

Insurance coverage, any changes, claims

Liens (equipment, tax, etc.)

Off-balance-sheet items, vacation, sick pay, and so on plus proprietary information, such as drawings and reverse-engineered and manufactured parts

Appendix D

Asset-Audit Requirements

I f your banker decides she wants an asset audit, you'll be asked to provide the auditor and buyer with the items listed below. This is usually done when there are high levels of accounts receivable and inventory included in the deal (and the bank's collateral).

Accounts Receivable (for all divisions, as applicable)

1. A detailed A/R aging as of two months from the most recent month closed. A sample of payments will be selected from this aging by reviewing invoices that are absent from it in comparison to the current aging.
2. Monthly cash receipts and sales journals for the last thirteen months closed.
3. A detail of credit memos issued during the most recent thirteen months closed. Depending on the results of other testing, a sample of credit memos may be picked for further testing.
4. Accounts receivable roll forward for each of the last thirteen months closed (beginning balance + sales – collections +/– debits/credits = end balance). Details will be needed for all cash received, discounts, credit memos, gross sales, and miscellaneous credits.

5. An accounts receivable aging will be needed as of the Friday before the start of the exam or the day of the exam. A sample of invoices will be selected from these accounts receivable aging. We will need to review the original invoice, bill of lading, and purchase orders to support the invoice selected.

6. Monthly summary A/R aging for the last thirteen months.

7. A listing of total sales for the company's top fifteen customers for the last thirteen months.

Inventory (for all divisions, as applicable)

1. Breakdown of the inventory by location, including address and dollar value. Please indicate if the location is leased or owned.

2. Breakdown of inventory by raw materials, work in progress, and finished goods from each location.

3. Reconciliation of latest physical inventory report to the general ledger and to the F/S.

4. Current insurance policy/certificate that covers all locations.

5. Monthly perpetual inventory report for the most recent thirteen months closed, which details inventory on hand by SKU by both quantity and amount. Please ensure it denotes raw materials, WIP, and finished goods.

6. Usage or sales history reports showing period's usage/sales for all SKUs, if available, over the last thirteen months.

7. Perpetual report as of the Friday before the start of the exam or the day before the exam.

8. A report or schedule showing the cost of completing the WIP inventory, if applicable.

9. Test counts will be performed at the more populated locations.

10. Cost test will be performed on a selected sample of the inventory.

11. A summary of adjustments made to inventory as a result of the three most recent test counts performed by internal personnel.

Accounts Payable

1. A/P aging for the last thirteen months closed.
2. Breakdown of accruals for the last month closed.
3. A/P reconciliation from the A/P aging to the general ledger and to the financial statement for the most current month closed.
4. Check registers for the most recent three months so that a sample of disbursements can be selected. Copies of the check or wire form, a copy of the vendor invoice, proof that the payment was cleared on the bank statement, and other documentation supporting the disbursement will be received for reasonableness.
5. A listing of the top fifteen vendors by total purchases for the past thirteen months.

Other

1. Balance sheet and P&L statements for the most recent three months closed.
2. Financial statements for the three most recent fiscal year-ends.
3. Taxes—federal and state payroll taxes, federal and state income taxes, real-estate taxes, personal property, and property taxes. Proof of payment is needed for the most recent month, quarter of year paid.
4. Latest three months of bank reconciliations, bank statements, and canceled checks for all cash accounts.
5. Month-end and weekly collateral report for the past thirteen months, if applicable.
6. General ledger—detail by month for the most recent thirteen months closed. Note—if general ledger is voluminous, please print the accounts receivable trade account; other accounts may be requested later. A summary trial balance will be required.
7. A copy of the insurance certificates supporting current insurance coverage. Proof of payment for the most recent period will also need to be reviewed.

APPENDIX E

Typical Asset Sale Contract Schedules

From Attorney Greg Russell with PRK Law in Bellevue, Washington, (425) 462-4700, grussell@prklaw.com:

Ref.	Reference #	Title
1.	Schedule 1.1	Acquired Assets - lists of specific tangible assets to be included in the sale, usually including accounts receivable, inventory and equipment as of the closing
2.	Schedule 1.2	Excluded Assets - list of assets to be excluded from the sale, such as personal vehicles or other assets unrelated to the business being purchased but which have been included over time on the Seller's balance sheet
3.	Schedule 1.3	Assumed Liabilities – list of business liabilities that the Buyer will assume at closing
4.	Schedule 1.4	Retained Liabilities – list of specific liabilities of the business that Seller will retain and pay at or after closing
5.	Schedule 1.5	Purchase Price Allocation – allocation of transaction consideration among different tax and asset classes
6.	Schedule 1.6	Jurisdictions/Qualifications/Permits – list of Seller's jurisdiction where formed, and states or other jurisdictions where Seller is required to be registered and qualified to do business, and other permits required by the business
7.	Schedule 1.7	Seller Equity – description of the authorized and outstanding equity of the Seller, any equity option plans or rights to acquire Seller equity
8.	Schedule 1.8	Liens or Encumbrances – list of all existing liens or encumbrances on Acquired Assets
9.	Schedule 1.9	Notices, Consents or Approvals – list of all notices, consents or approvals required to be obtained from a governmental entity or third person in connection with the sale, including consents needed for the assignment of any material contracts from the Seller to the Buyer.
10.	Schedule 1.10	Financial Statements – attach financial statements (balance sheet, income statement, statements of cash flow) for specified number of prior years, and the portion of the current year prior to closing of the sale.
11.	Schedule 1.11	Undisclosed Liabilities – list of any liabilities that are not reflected or reserved for on the Seller's balance sheet, or current liabilities that were not incurred in the ordinary course of Seller's business
12.	Schedule 1.12	Absence of Changes – describe any material adverse changes to the Seller or the business since the last audited financial statement
13.	Schedule 1.13	Legal Compliance – describe any situations where Seller or the business is not in compliance with any federal, state or local statutes or regulations
14.	Schedule 1.14	Employees – list detailed information about all employees, including copies of any employment or compensation agreements, or summaries of any verbal agreements; employee census, current compensation and increases in compensation in

[1] https://www.zacks.com/stock/news/181853/15-memorable-investing-quotes-from-warren-buffett

[2] www.charleswarner.us/articles/WarrenBuffett_EBITDA.doc

[3] http://www.valuewalk.com/2016/11/warren-buffett-not-believe-ebitda/

[4] https://www.forbes.com/sites/brentbeshore/2014/11/13/ebitda-is-bs-earnings/#74791bcf6070

INDEX

ABOUT THE AUTHOR

J ohn Martinka is known as the "Escape Artist" because of the work he does in three areas:

1. Dramatically increasing the value of companies via growth by acquisition
2. Creating large exits for small businesses so the owner can leave the business with style, grace, and more money
3. Helping executives escape the corporate world by buying the right business the right way

John has over twenty years' worth of business experience as an intermediary, was a cofounder of "Partner" On-Call Network, and has helped over one hundred clients successfully navigate the treacherous waters of buy-sell transactions. He was awarded board approval in business acquisitions and sales by the Society for Advancement of Consulting, LLC. He currently serves on two for-profit company boards.

John works with numerous nonprofits and twice was a Rotary Club president. In 2005, he started a Rotary project titled Improving Education through Technology in Conjunction with the Newport High School (Bellevue, Washington) Cisco Networking Academy to install computer labs in schools. As of this publishing, over three thousand computers have been donated and installed in Slovakia, Turkey, and Antigua and Barbuda, with the students doing most of the on-site work.

The team has gone to Antigua nine times and has also distributed nine thousand dictionaries to third-grade students, provided and installed a video-teleconferencing system between Antigua and Barbuda, and recently started a program to train teachers on how to teach more effectively by using technology. John's wife, Jan, has set up six sewing centers in Antigua to teach women living in a high-poverty area the skill of sewing, which they use to make their families' clothes, school uniforms, and items they can sell.

Find out more about John and the services he offers by going to www. martinkaconsulting.com. You can reach him at john@johnmartinka. com or 425-576-1814.

Made in the USA
San Bernardino, CA
30 March 2018